The Human Legacy

THE
HUMAN
LEGACY

LEON FESTINGER

New York   Columbia University Press   *1983*

Library of Congress Cataloging in Publication Data

Festinger, Leon, 1919–
The human legacy.

Bibliography: p.
Includes index.
1. Human evolution.   2. Social evolution.   I. Title.
GN281.F474   1983   573.2   82-22178
ISBN 0-231-05672-9
ISBN 0-231-05673-7 (pbk.)

COLUMBIA UNIVERSITY PRESS
New York   Guildford, Surrey

CONTENTS

Preface

MANY PEOPLE helped me in one way or another in pursuing the work that has led to this book. I want to thank them and express my appreciation.

To begin with, there are Joe Greenbaum, then Dean of the Graduate Faculty of the New School for Social Research, and Jack Everett, then President of the New School. When I told them that I intended to close my laboratory and start learning about archeology, neither of them blinked an eye; they actually encouraged me. They must have thought that anything would be better than what I had been doing.

More encouragement came from Sherry Washburn, who had himself contributed so much in the area I wanted to pursue. He not only thought it was good for me to become interested in these things, but I also learned a great deal from him. There were also a few psychologists for whom I have great respect, who not only didn't think I had gone off the deep end but even became interested and participated with me in highly instructive seminars. These are Mike Gazzaniga, Julian Hochberg, George Miller, Serge Moscovici, and Dave Premack.

There are limits to what one can grasp and understand just from reading. There is much in any field that does not get written down or that is difficult to convey with language alone. So, I have also on occasion sought to talk with experts and to visit some excavations with them. There are three from whom I learned enormous amounts: Ofer Bar-Yosef, Arthur Jelinek, and Jacques Tixier.

Four people read and criticized an earlier draft of the manuscript: Liz Coleman, Jack Everett, Stanley Schachter and, perforce, Trudy Festinger. Good, honest, and constructive criticism is hard to come by but all four supplied it.

One more person must be mentioned here: Sallie Marx, who put up gracefully with my endless revisions, my snarling about typos, and my dumping many of the chores about the bibliography on her shoulders.

Finally, my thanks to the Sloan Foundation for having facilitated my education in the matters that form the basis of this book.

Introduction

FOUR YEARS AGO I closed my laboratory which, over time, had become devoted to studying ever narrowing aspects of how the human eye moves. It is natural for me to talk as if the laboratory was at fault, but a laboratory is only a collection of rooms and equipment. It was I who conceived of, and worked on, narrower and narrower technical problems.

That is not a proper occupation for an aging man who resents that adjective. Young men and women should work on narrow problems. Young people become enthusiastic easily: any new finding is an exciting thing. Older people have too much perspective on the past and, perhaps, too little patience with the future. Very few small discoveries turn out to be important over the years; things that would have sent me jumping and shouting in my youth now left me calm and judgmental. And my lack of enthusiasm kept reminding me of that despised adjective, aging.

Having a critical perspective on the recent past is debilitating in other ways also. I have been actively engaged in research in the field of psychology for more than forty years and during that time have worked on statistics, studied the behavior of animals, worked on decision processes and motivation, proposed theories about social behavior, and explored visual perception. Along with me, many other talented and active people have done research and filled the journals with technical articles in these fields and more. Indeed, these forty years have covered an extraordinarily active period in psychology generally.

Forty years in my own life seems like a long time to me, and while some things have been learned about human beings and human behavior during this time, progress has not been rapid enough; nor has the new knowledge been impressive enough. And even worse, from a broader point of view, we do not seem to have been working on many of the important problems.

Let us take a look at this curious animal, the modern human being, to ask if we really know much about him or are we simply accustomed to, and adapted to, his peculiarities. Just superficial reflection reveals many facets of human activity that seem very strange. One striking thing about us is that we have no natural habitat. Other animals live and prosper best under relatively specific climatic conditions, but we do not seem to care. We flourish all over this planet. If we once had a natural habitat, has its loss affected our thoughts, emotions, and patterns of behavior, or doesn't it matter?

Another strange thing is the amount of energy, work, and time we devote to aesthetic activities: decoration, color, visual art, music, dance, poetry. Yet there is no major body of knowledge or theory that we could call a Psychology of Aesthetics. We seem to have almost totally ignored an area of important human concern.

Equally strange is our general addiction to games, both physical and mental. The profusion of games is truly startling: card games, board games, word games, ball games, electronic games. Some games are entirely dominated by chance, others mix chance and skill, while still others are games of complete knowledge in which only skill matters. Some games are competitive; others are played alone. We even assemble in huge crowds to watch others playing games. What does all this mean? Do we simply get easily bored and cannot tolerate inactivity? I can find nothing in the literature of scientific psychology that helps me to understand such bizarre behavior.

Looked at from a purely evolutionary point of view, that is, the capacities, characteristics, and proclivities that enhance the survival possibilities of the species, the human carries quite a bit of useless excess baggage. Moreover, he cherishes this excess baggage—to him it is not a burden but a source of pleasure. If anyone wants to pursue the unedifying quest for differences between humans and other animals, the human activities connected with this cherished baggage is the place to look. It is not difficult to imagine why issues such as this have been shunned by the science of psychology. Wedded to quantitative measurement and experimental methodology, more or less in the image of the natural sciences, such issues are difficult to approach.

So I closed my laboratory, deserted experimental methodology, and decided that I wanted to learn whatever I could about humans by searching for origins in prehistory. How did humans evolve? What were the beginnings of our present way of life? What were the origins of human societies that today face so many problems? In short, I embarked upon a thoroughly unfocused, almost unbounded, pursuit. I cannot even try to specify what I was pursuing. If this endeavor seems crazy, I want to assure you that it was highly pleasurable insanity.

In the last few years I have learned many things that I did not know before: about humans who lived two million years ago; about the techniques of making stone tools; about the earliest beginnings of art; about the circumstances in which humans settled down to live in one place all year round; about the origins of agriculture and the development of organized societies. I have learned by reading indiscriminately and by talking with many people who were experts and were discriminating.

Coming to such a task with my background, it is natural that the questions I asked myself and the facts that I found interesting were ones that bordered on the social and psychological. Most of the data, however, did not lend themselves easily to inferences about such questions. Reading long, detailed accounts of the shape, size, and style of the stone tools uncovered at some site, for example, benefited me little. Although I tried to learn about and understand the data and the techniques, I have certainly not succeeded very well. There is too much to learn. If I visited a site that was being excavated, it remained largely meaningless to me until the excavator told me what to look at and what it meant. I can only hope that I have not made too many errors of fact and interpretation.

The developments over a period of more than three million years from the first fully bipedal primates until the appearance of modern man about forty thousand years ago are revealed primarily in fossil bones and stone tools. The prehistory of modern man left a much more varied record—art, houses, pottery, and more. The strands that might weave it together are multiple and tangled, many of them still hidden. Possibly, because of the sparseness of the data, no totally coherent pattern of evolution, change, and development will ever appear.

What I have tried to do, while stuffing my head with facts and data, was to pick up a thread here and a thread there, threads that seemed to me to show some continuity over that huge period of time, threads that could help me understand how we arrived where we are today. The chapters in this book contain the variety of ideas that I managed to pick up and hold onto.

I have grappled, I fear unsuccessfully, with one persistent problem. I cannot, and do not want to, rid myself of the conviction that ideas, hypotheses, and guesses must maintain a close relationship to empirical data. I do not talk here about proof or disproof—this is almost never attainable. But at least the data should constrain the interpretations and the interpretations should carry implications about new data. Otherwise, one may be concocting fascinating tales, tales which may suit our predispositions, but, nevertheless, are only tales. And imaginative humans can easily make up stories and yarns.

The paleontological and archaeological record is rather unfriendly to the kind of thinking I like to do. There is almost nothing that cannot, with seemingly equal plausibility, be viewed in a variety of ways, some diametrically opposed to others. The scarcity and incompleteness of data, and the lurking fact that what we do know is limited by where someone decided to dig, makes for an ambiguity that frequently remains unresolved.

I have tried to keep interpretations, those borrowed from others as well as those emerging from my own ideas, in touch with and constrained by the known facts. But I realize that in many instances alternative interpretations are not only possible, but easily supplied. I have, of course, explicated the facts and the contexts that led me to the explanations that I offer. I must admit, however, that not only do I present an unintegrated set of causes and continuities, but what I present is, in the end, what seems most plausible to me.

I have purposely avoided, wherever possible, using anthropological data about modern groups to support interpretations about the past. There are many who do this, but it seems risky and unwarranted to me. Modern groups, no matter how simple or "primitive" their social organization, their life style, or their belief systems, are not equivalent to human groups that lived twenty thousand, or even ten thousand years ago. Biologically they are the same, and if one wants to make biological inferences, one can exploit the anthropological data. But psychologically and socially there is no reason in the world to believe modern groups can be equated with groups of very long ago. An additional ten or twenty thousand years has elapsed during which societal forms and life styles may have changed; groups such as these are highly selected either because they have been isolated or because, for some reason, they have resisted the dominant trends in human societies; such groups also, generally, live in marginal locations into which they have been pushed by the "more developed" societies.

So if modern groups that live by hunting and gathering, rather than agriculture, usually have a division of labor between the sexes in which the men hunt and the women gather, this does not mean that it was that way 20,000 years ago. At best it indicates that this is one possible means of organization of work that humans may employ. If modern pastoral, nomadic groups resist efforts to induce them to settle down, this does not mean that 10,000 years ago humans resisted sedentary existence. Magical and religious beliefs held by simple modern groups are no indication of what beliefs were held by humans in the very remote past.

I do not want to be misinterpreted; I certainly do not think that the study of modern groups is without value. At a minimum they have enriched the variety of speculations about the past by pointing to the great cultural diversity that is possible. However, interpretations of the past must be based primarily on data about the past, sometimes with an eye on the sequence of events; that is, understanding of occurrences 10,000 years ago can be profitably guided by knowledge of what had evolved by 9,000 years ago. But the best we can do with knowledge about modern groups is to view it as indicating a *possible* means of adaptation by humans.

I cannot pretend that this book is exhaustive—it is not. It covers neither the entirety of human evolution and development, nor does it deal with all the available data. The selectivity in what I do cover stems from a variety of considerations. First of all, I have ignored or dealt only tangentially with data from many parts of the world. In describing developments, and trying to explain them, I have usually limited myself to data from those areas where those developments started. For example, agriculture spread to Europe between one and two thousand years after it had started in western Asia. To understand how and why it started, one must, then, look at western Asia, not Europe. The consequence is that at different times and for different topics I talk about different parts of the inhabited world. I have tried not to allow this to distort the accounts; I hope I have succeeded. I think that I am talking not just about humans in this place or that place but about humans generally.

There is a major omission that exists for a different reason. I have ignored the wealth of archaeological data on the American Indian. In the course of trying to absorb what is known and what is conjectured about the last three and a half million years. I have periodically been forced to set some boundaries so as to make my task possible. Where I have explored, I have tried to learn enough to be able to make my own evaluations of interpretations in the existing literature. That's a lot of information to acquire. The most severe restriction I enforced on myself was to stay away from data on the American Indian. They appear later in prehistory and nothing is known about continuity into the past; they lived in different circumstances and in isolation from the developments in the rest of the world. This omission may be a big mistake. If data from American Indians can produce additional insights into some of the problems I discuss, or cast doubt on some of my interpretations, I trust someone will tell me.

The book is also limited by the ideas in the literature that I found convincing and by the ideas that occurred to me that survived my self-criticism. I did not want to write chapters in which I merely said that little was known, some say this, some say that, and I myself do not know what to say. Fragmentary as it is, I hope that the book introduces some better understanding of what kind of an organism the human is and how we developed the way of life we now "enjoy."

I have organized the remaining chapters into two parts which have different objectives. The first part is an attempt to infer something about the "nature of the beast" from the evolutionary record. Every animal has innate characteristics that are genetically determined and it seems to me that we should be able to learn something about such human characteristics by examining the directions of biological evolution and the conditions under which it took place. I have certainly not tried to describe the totality of "human nature," that nasty phrase, but to speculate wherever I could about some characteristics that I felt one was almost forced to assume if one were to understand anything at all.

The second part of the book deals mainly with the last twenty or thirty thousand years before the present, a period in which there are no discernible evolutionary changes. Modern man, the species of human being that now exists, did not always live the way we do. The patterns of life style and social organization have gone through enormous changes in the last fifteen thousand years. I have tried to examine, in the hope that it may add to our understanding of human beings and human society today, how and why this species, with the innate characteristics that I think it possesses, initiated these changes. How did it come about that human groups settled down to live in one place and changed from depending on wild plants and animals to agriculture? What are the origins of some of the belief systems that are so widely held today? Where are the beginnings of large, highly stratified, societies?

Needless to say, it is impossible for any person to examine and interpret the past, without being inordinately influenced by the belief system and the values that he has grown up with and lived with. I think it is also necessary, in order to interpret the past adequately, to separate oneself from precisely those things that it is impossible to discard. And so, obviously, the endeavor here is not successful. Archimedes is reputed to have declared that if he had a lever long enough, a fulcrum strong enough, and presumably a place far enough away to stand, he could move the world. I would only wish for the third of these requirements: a place far enough away to stand so that I could see human society clearly.

The Human Legacy

PART ONE
THE NARROW PATH OF EVOLUTION

CHAPTER ONE
The Earliest Humans

THIS book is about humans. How did they evolve and develop—physically, socially, psychologically—into the modern version of the species that we see around us today, living in complex societies, their lives littered with problems? To decide where to begin telling this story, we must first decide on some characteristic or quality that would lead us to say unhesitatingly that a certain animal is human.

This is not the same problem as trying to specify the evolutionary line through which modern man came into being. There is fairly general agreement that somewhere between five and fifteen million years ago (a span of time chosen to be long enough to enable such agreement) two evolutionary lines separated—one leading to today's human and the other to the modern nonhuman primates. There are many who go so far as to identify an animal that existed way back then, Ramapithecus, as the likely beginning of the human evolutionary line. This identification rests on the shape of its jawbone and the greater dominance of molar teeth. Jawbones and teeth seem to survive best, and no other part of Ramapithecus has ever been found—jaws and teeth are all we know. No one, however, seems to show the slightest inclination to attribute human characteristics to Ramapithecus. The shape of the human jawbone and the pitiful condition of the modern human's teeth are hardly characteristics that we consider important (not counting the opinions of dentists). Perhaps Ramapithecus also had other characteristics that we would consider more important, but we simply do not know.

What characteristics in an animal would persuade us to call it "human"? Clearly, it has little to do with genetic similarity. At least 98 percent of the structural genes are identical in modern man and modern chimpanzee, yet no one wants to call the latter "human." There are characteristics that we think of as "peculiarly human" and those are the ones we would like to identify in, or infer from, the fossil record in order to say: "This is the earliest human."

Almost four million years ago there already existed animals that walked only on two legs—animals that, in some physical aspects, had a resemblance to the modern human. Such animals may have existed earlier, of course, but the earliest fossil evidence that we have is dated to about that time. That is a long time ago and it is difficult to absorb fully how long ago it was. The problem is somewhat like comprehending a national budget of something like 700 billion dollars. It has no direct meaning in our experience or in our thoughts. Modern man, as we know him today, appeared on the scene only forty thousand years ago—and that is also a long period of time.

What were these animals of four million years ago like, and are they reasonable candidates for the elevated designation of "human"? Standing erect, they were, perhaps, between 4 and 5 feet in height. The cranial capacity, reflecting the size of the brain (but not necessarily its effectiveness), was about one-fourth that of the human of today. The hand had an opposable thumb but its length and separation from the other fingers place it somewhere between that of modern man and modern chimpanzee. The strongest similarity to modern man was the fully erect bipedal posture. They did not walk sometimes on two legs and other times on four, as modern chimpanzees, for example, do. They did not walk stooping over as if they were emerging into bipedalism. The entire skeletal structure indicates that they walked fully erect—just as we walk today (Johanson and White 1979; Johanson 1980). Perhaps even more persuasive evidence of this is the spectacular unearthing of footprints left by some of these four-million-year-ago animals. The shape and form of these prints and the areas where weight was supported are almost indistinguishable from our own footprints (White 1980).

So do we want to call them human? Does the physical characteristic of fully erect bipedalism have any greater importance than the shape of a jaw and a relative preponderance of molar teeth? Many of us are used to the idea that when man freed his hands from the encumbrance of locomotion this was a great evolutionary event. We immediately see him making tools, throwing spears, and writing sonnets. But if we look at it carefully, bipedalism, in and of itself, must have been a nearly disastrous disadvantage.

Speed of movement, for example, for attack or defense or escape, would have been a highly advantageous thing for any animal. Bipedalism greatly reduced the speed of movement. As Washburn pointed out to me (personal communication) the most talented and highly trained modern men, running under ideal conditions, are able to run a distance of one mile at a rate of only 15 miles an hour. Many species of four-legged animals can easily sustain speeds of about 35 miles an hour under ordinary conditions. Almost any four-legged animal can run faster than a man. Using the free limbs to climb trees to escape would, to some extent, have offset the vulnerability caused by the lack of speed. In any event, however, partial bipedalism as represented in the modern chimpanzee, for example, would be much more advantageous. Such an animal can use all four limbs for running when it wants to and can also climb very effectively.

Full bipedalism also has additional heavy costs. Nonhuman primates, many of which are partially bipedal, do reasonably well on three legs while a wound or a fracture is healing—a wound or fracture that would, four million years ago, have been fatal to a fully bipedal creature. Washburn is correct in insisting that "the evolution of a locomotor pattern that [increases vulnerability] and reduces speed needs special explanation" (personal communication).

The important thing that allowed this seriously handicapped species to survive and even flourish is not that two arms were left free for other possible uses, but that the animal had to be equipped with a brain and a neural system that enabled him to employ fruitfully and adaptively these otherwise potentially useless appendages. Bipedal animals that evolved without the adequate accompanying neural basis (let's call it intelligence) would not have survived very long except in rather special circumstances. It is difficult to see how two relatively useless arms help the kangaroo, for example. Or how two useless wings help the emu, or the ostrich, or the penguin.

To what use did our fully bipedal primates put these free limbs so many years ago? Lee (1979) and also Lovejoy (1981) point out that the hands and arms could have been used for carrying food and for carrying the infant child. And they both attribute great importance to this, speculating that it permitted food sharing and social organization that also helped overcome the physical handicap of bipedalism. They are probably correct; carrying could have been important, and cooperative social organization could certainly have contributed its share. But these were not the only things—the arms and hands were not, and are not, specialized appendages as, for example, the legs of man are. An extraordinary variety of uses were invented for the arms and hands—and invented is the key word.

Thus, a part of an animal's body became a truly multipurpose instrument, a rather unusual occurrence. One could say that many animals use limbs for more than one purpose, and it is true that they do. A horse, for example, sometimes uses its rear legs to kick as well as their primary function of enabling movement. Dogs sometimes use their legs to scratch and dig. Chimpanzees use their forelimbs to carry things, throw things, reach for things. But there is a startling difference in degree, in the variety of uses invented for the human forelimbs. Indeed, the inventive human has even tried to turn his hind limbs into multipurpose instruments. The foot does a lot of work when we drive cars, for example. There is no animal for whom the biology dictates multipurpose use of a limb—it is the inventive brain that enables it. The species survived, and evolved further, because this animal with its 350 to 400 cubic centimeter brain had the capacity to explore, to invent, to be ingenious. That mental capacity surely labels the species as human. From that point, with an animal that could and did invent, does the story start.

From that time on the directions of successful evolutionary development for this species were narrowly limited. Biological changes that increased the usefulness of these limbs could provide ever-increasing adaptational advantages, but such possible biological changes were few in number. Changes in the size and organization of the brain which would increase the inventiveness and ingenuity of the human is one; changes in the hand, and in the hand-brain connections, which could increase the ability to exert fine manual control is another.

What else? The visual system could evolve toward greater acuity and better binocular depth perception. This could increase the usefulness of the hands, and perhaps such evolution did occur. We do not know and, probably, will never know. Changes in size, greater strength, ability to run faster—any such changes would have only minor impact on the ability of the human to feed itself and protect itself from danger. Some such changes did, indeed, occur. The human did become larger and Neanderthal man, for example, was even larger and stronger than modern man. But this was largely irrelevant to adaptational advantage. Being able to throw a spear a little harder would provide a negligible advantage in comparison with being able to manufacture a better spear or being able to invent an accurate mechanical spear thrower. Actually, increased size is a mixed blessing for any animal. A larger animal may possess some survival advantages but a larger animal also has to supply more fuel to the system—he has to obtain and eat more food. For the human, increased size has never done much; for the human, it is perhaps analogous to evolutionary changes that would enable hawks or eagles to walk more rapidly on the ground.

The hand and the brain did evolve. Over the course of millions of years the brain grew larger and, presumably, changed in organization; the hand became more and more capable of performing actions involving fine precision (Napier 1962). Thus, the human, forced by a physical handicap to rely on inventiveness and ingenuity, determined the direction of its own evolution.

We should be clear about the nature of the argument that has been developed. There is, of course, no direct evidence that these animals were more imaginative, more ingenious, or more creative than any other animal of that time. We do know that they were fully bipedal and we know that fully bipedal primates continued to exist and still exist today. We have argued that bipedalism is a serious physical handicap for an animal and that a species with such a characteristic would not have survived unless something else adequately compensated for the handicap. We have also argued that the most important compensating characteristics would have been ingenuity and inventiveness in finding uses for the forelimbs.

How did these very early humans live? Where did they live? What were they like? The evidence on the basis of which one can try to answer such questions is, as one might expect, limited. The evidence consists of bones that have been found, the locations in which they have been found, and geological evidence concerning the geography and climate of that time. The fact that we can say anything at all about them is, in itself, a tribute to the ingenuity of the modern human.

First of all, how do we know how old those bones are? The problems of determining the age of rocks or fossils are enormous, and it is only in the last twenty years that significant, even remarkable, progress has been made in establishing reasonably reliable, absolute dating methods. Even so, we cannot expect accurate dating of such old fossils to the century, or even to the millennium. Plus or minus a few hundred thousand years is impressive enough. And so we know that these oldest humans lived between four and three million years ago.

The very earliest human fossils have all been found in East Africa—central and southern Ethiopia, northern Kenya, and Tanzania. As far as we can tell, this area represented a rather special and benign place during the long period from five million to two million years ago. The climate of the earth had been progressively cooling for a considerable time. By four million years ago glaciation had developed and glaciers covered the Antarctic continent and the high mountain ranges of middle latitudes. Very marked cyclical changes repeatedly occurred over much of the planet, each lasting for tens of thousands of years. During cold glacial periods the mean annual temperature in the middle latitudes would have been between 0° and 3° C. (32° and 37° F.), perhaps, while in the warmer interglacial periods it would have reached perhaps 5° or 6° C (41° or 43° F.). These are large temperature changes and such oscillations have continued to today. Geologists consider that we are now living in an interglacial period that started only about twenty thousand years ago.

But these general events were only minimally reflected in the areas in which these early humans lived. That area does not reveal evidence of cyclical temperature fluctuations, although lake and ocean levels and humidity would have been affected by the glaciation that occurred in other parts of the world. During periods of heavy glaciation water levels would have been lower. Butzer summarizes the climatic conditions in the area as follows:

> It is perhaps not fortuitous that the key focus of hominid [human] evolution during the Pliocene and early Pleistocene [5 million to 1 million years ago] was eastern and southern Africa, an area least affected by the large-scale environmental dislocations of the end-Tertiary. Here we find increasingly large populations of taxonomically diverse hominids in overlapping geographical ranges, at present documented between 27°S and 9°N latitudes. (1977:575)

As Butzer says, by 1.5 million years ago humans had spread throughout eastern and southern Africa. It was not just one species— there were at least two fully bipedal species that existed simultaneously. Evolutionary biological changes also took place—the species that existed 3.5 million years ago no longer existed 1.5 million years ago. They had been replaced by others.

The spread of these early humans, over the course of some two million years, through an area about 2,000 miles in extent, does not, of course, represent rapid population growth or very rapid expansion. Two million years is a long time; the movement in each few generations could have been very small indeed, hardly noticeable. Nor does it represent an expansion of early human groups into new climates. The spread was confined to an area with rather similar environmental conditions. The area was characterized, during that period, by reasonable temperatures together with a semi-arid climate—alternating wet and dry seasons of the year. The sites that have been discovered were not far from water sources—lakeshore, stream, or sinkhole, for example—and in areas between open and closed vegetation. Thus, they lived in proximity to a wide variety of plant and animal life. Their diet was undoubtedly similarly varied, changing from season to season.

The likelihood is that they lived in small groups, moving their location from time to time to satisfy their requirements for food. Naturally, the evidence for such an assertion is very meager. One can try to infer group size from the size of a campsite, but to do this adequately one must make assumptions concerning how long the site was occupied. And if we are primarily concerned, as we are here, with the period before three million years ago, we must admit that we are engaged in relatively unrestricted speculation. The best available evidence comes from a remarkable excavation in Ethiopia, where fossil bones were uncovered from a number of individuals dating back to more than three million years ago (Johanson and White 1979). Bones from almost all parts of the body are represented among these fossils and "in several cases there are associated skeletal parts of the same individual." Indeed, nearly 40 percent of the skeleton of one person has been recovered. It reveals an upright, adult, bipedal animal, no more than 4 feet tall, and presumed to be female. The males are guessed to be, perhaps, 4.5 to 5 feet tall. These bones represent at least 35 different individuals, probably more, possibly as many as 65. If there were indications of near simultaneous death, this would mean that fairly sizable groups of humans lived in proximity to each other. But there are no such indications; the collection of many bones probably represent repeated occupations of the same area over many generations. If the latter interpretation is correct, then it would mean that these earliest humans did not continually roam from place to place, but rather stayed in one place for appreciable periods of time and, probably, returned annually.

One would like to be able to say more about these earliest humans but, if one wants to stay even remotely in touch with evidence, there is little more to say—except for one very important thing. They must have already invented various uses for the two unencumbered hands and arms. They may very well have used them for carrying food, but if they did, except for occasional large pieces of meat, perhaps, it would not have been a major use. Efficient carrying of appreciable quantities of foods would have required the invention of carrying devices fulfilling the functions of a container. Imagine trying to carry water, fruits, nuts, berries, or edible roots without such a device. Not much could be carried at any one time. It may have been too early for such an invention—but maybe not.

But one thing we do know and can state with some confidence. They used their hands to manipulate tools. What these tools were, and their specific uses, we also do not know. They may have used broken pieces of wood or bone—these would not have survived so many millions of years. They may have used pieces of rock—if such have survived one would not recognize that, long ago, a human had used it as a tool.

Then how can one know that they used tools? Because we know that they realized the advantage of having a sharp-edged or pointed object. And how can we be sure of that? Because excavations in Ethiopia (Lewin 1981) have revealed that about 2.6 million years ago humans were manufacturing stone tools deliberately, creating sharp edges. And it is unimaginable that sharp edges would be deliberately created unless the manufacturers had already realized how useful they were.

If one claims that the constraints on human evolution were different from other animals—that the only materially advantageous genetic changes for the human were ones that increased cognitive capacity, creativity, ingenuity, and enabled their expression—then it is perhaps useful to show that humans are different from other animals. This does not involve demonstrating that there is a sharp discontinuity between humans and any other animal. It merely involves showing that in relevant areas the differences that exist are very, very great.

One would think that this is so obvious that it would be trivially easy to demonstrate to everyone's satisfaction. It turns out not to be so easy because some remarkably strong emotional reactions seem to be evoked by the issue, reactions that continually attempt to blur the distinction between large differences and discontinuities. Since we are here concerned with very early humans, the most relevant area to examine is the exercise of ingenuity and inventiveness in the use and manufacture of tools.

Do animals other than the human use tools in ingenious ways? Of course they do—the human is not the sole possessor of ingenuity. It has been widely known since Köhler (1927) published his observations on chimpanzees that these animals used tools. For example, one chimpanzee, without instruction, without demonstration, without hints or clues, fitted two sticks together lengthwise so that, with the resulting longer stick he could reach and get a banana that was otherwise out of reach. Someone might point out that this chimpanzee was fortunate that the sticks, supplied by a human, were able to easily fit together lengthwise. But this misses the point. The chimpanzee had sufficient ingenuity to create and use this simple tool.

But tool use and manufacture are not confined to chimpanzees or other higher primates. Beck has recently performed a great service by publishing what is probably, to date, an exhaustive catalogue of nonhuman tool use and manufacture. A few examples should suffice to give a picture of how extensive such activities are.

A number of species of myrmicine ants have devised tools for carrying and transporting soft foods such as honey, fruit pulp, or the body fluids of prey. They place a bit of leaf or wood into or over the liquid food. They then wait a while until the soft food has been absorbed by the carrying tool, and then bring it back to the colony where others can feed on it. It is estimated that "a worker can retrieve approximately 10 times as much food (by weight) using a tool than it can carry in its crop" (Beck 1980:16).

Egyptian vultures apparently like ostrich eggs and, in Tanzania, have been observed to use stones to break open such eggs. The vultures find a stone, some weighing in the neighborhood of 500 grams, carry the stone in their bill to the egg, sometimes over distances of 10 meters or so, and then break the egg by repeated hurling or pounding with the stone. "Eggs were broken with 4 to 12 hits in periods ranging from two to eight minutes" (p. 24).

Woodpecker finches use twigs or other suitable material to probe for insects in holes or under bark, places they cannot reach directly. They hold the tool in their bills and if they find an insect, pry it out or catch it as it tries to escape. One bird was even observed to "not only pick up or detach a tool object, but would also shorten it or subtract bits that impeded its insertion" (p. 26).

Sea otters seem to use tools rather habitually. They find suitable rocks on the ocean floor, bring them up, and use them for pounding mollusks, mussels, and other seafood to break the shell. They even use stones to pound abalone sufficiently to detach it from a rock so they can eat it. If a sea otter finds a very good rock, he may carry it with him for a considerable period of time, even on land. It has also been reported that sea otters "attach strands of kelp to their bodies to add buoyancy and stability during prolonged periods of floating rest or sleep" (p. 44).

If we move to the inevitable chimpanzee, we find, of course, a considerable variety of tool use. The chimp uses pounding tools; in the wild, in West Africa, numerous observers have reported that they use stones, or even sticks, to pound open seeds and nuts. The chimp uses probing tools; grass blades, twigs, or other suitable material are inserted as a probe into a termite nest. They wait for termites to seize the probe, and then withdraw it and eat the termites. The probing tool must be flexible but strong and resilient, and it is clear that "considerable knowledge and skill are required to locate and expose workable tunnels, select and manufacture tools and utilize the tools effectively" (p. 87). In some locations chimps have been observed to use twigs to fish for ants or to obtain honey from the nest of a bee. The chimp clearly manufactures tools. They are widely known to chew leaves briefly in order to crumple them and increase their ability to absorb water. The crumpled leaves are then used as sponges for a variety of purposes. The chimp even manufactures tools with sharp edges; "chimpanzees chewed splinters from the end of a stick to produce a chisel-shaped edge that was used for prying" (p. 114).

And so it is clear that the human is not unique in the use and manufacture of tools. It should also be simultaneously clear that there is an enormous difference of degree, both in the variety of tool uses and in the dependence on tools for survival, between the human and other animals.

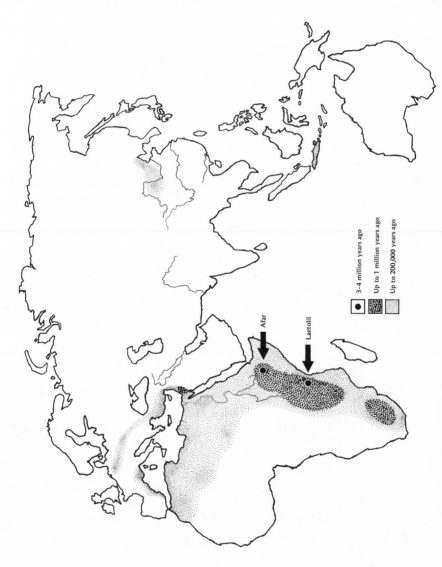

Map 1 Distribution of Early Man. Some of the major areas inhabited by early humans.

3-4 million years ago
Up to 1 million years ago
Up to 200,000 years ago

Afar

Laetolil

CHAPTER TWO
From Tool Use to Technology

Mᴏʀᴇ than two and a half million years ago some early humans had a fantastic, new idea. The essence of that idea seems simple to us today, but it was of monumental significance at that time. It was not necessary to limit themselves to using, as tools, objects that ordinarily were naturally available in their environment. They could, instead, create objects that were not ordinarily available. If, for example, there was a need for a piece of stone with a sharp edge to cut meat or animal skin or wood, they could try to manufacture such an object.

We do not know how many kinds of material they tried to use to manufacture such objects—the variety must have been considerable. We only know with certainty that they tried to manufacture stone tools with sharp edges because, eventually, they succeeded. The earliest, deliberately manufactured stone tools date back to about two and a half million years ago, but rather few have been found that are that old. By two million years ago, however, there was clearly in existence a widespread, well-developed stone tool industry.

Creating a useful sharp edge on a piece of stone is not an easy thing to do, unless one knows how. The knowledge that had to be acquired and the problems that had to be solved in order to "know how" reveal something about the intellect of these humans. It is well to emphasize that it reveals something about the intellect of the earliest humans that we talked about in the preceding chapter. These tools were manufactured by humans at a time at least 500,000 years before there is the first evidence of a new human species with significantly greater cranial capacity. Perhaps, as new evidence accumulates, as new fossil remains are found from the period between three and two million years ago, the beginning of increase in cranial capacity may be pushed back in time, but probably not far. Most likely, these early tools were manufactured by humans with cranial capacities of not more than about 400 to 450 cc.

If you or I were given the task, today, of making a sharp stone edge, what would we do?—barring instruction and books. Just picking up a rock and somehow smashing it will not work. Every once in a while a sharp edge might emerge by chance, but not in a reliable, repeatable way.

First, you will have to discover what kind of stone to use and what not to use. Fine grained silicon-based stone is best for the purpose— chert, flint, or obsidian, a naturally occurring, volcanically produced glass. Such rocks, if one strikes them properly, fracture in a predictable manner and produce very sharp edges.

Even after you know this, and are able to identify the proper rock to begin with, you would still have trouble. You now have to discover how to prepare a place on the rock to strike and the proper direction and angle of the blow with a hammerstone in order to flake off the desired part in the desired place. Once you know all of this, only considerable practice will develop the motor skill needed. This may all sound difficult enough, starting with no knowledge about it at all, but the complexity of the discovery and inventive process is even greater. How, if you do not know the proper manner in which to strike the stone, is it possible to determine what is, or is not, a suitable type of stone to use?

It is difficult, perhaps impossible, to give an adequate and complete verbal description that would enable you or me to begin to manufacture stone tools of even the most primitive kind. The first time that I watched an expert lithic technologist, Jacques Tixier, make such tools was considerably more instructive than anything I had learned from a considerable amount of reading on the subject: the ringing sound that came from a good piece of flint and the dull sound from a poor piece; watching him decide where to prepare the striking platform; seeing how he held the stone and how he struck it; my surprise to realize that the flake came off the bottom of the stone as he held it; the certainty with which he knew the size and shape of the flake that was to be produced.

The earliest makers of stone tools did not know all that is now known about the principles and the variety of techniques of manufacture. The earliest tools might be regarded as primitive. But let us not be fooled by that word. They are primitive only in comparison with much later, more sophisticated tools. The first inventors of stone tool manufacture had no one to observe or imitate. They had to originate the idea of deliberate manufacture, perhaps the greatest part of the achievement; they then had to try to do it, realize that some stones were better than others, and learn how to control the fracturing of the stone. They did not always use the best rocks, nor was the exe-

cution always excellent, but the tools were useful and the idea of
manufacturing things that are otherwise not available continued to
be the hallmark of the human, an adequate compensation for his
physical handicap.

We do not know how many hundreds of thousands of years elapsed
between the idea and the accumulation of sufficient knowledge to
make the idea executable. It might have taken a long time. If it did
take many, many generations, then we must assume that the species
we call human, that lived more than two and a half million years ago,
was able to transmit an idea that was not well executable from generation to generation. We also must assume, since first attempts would
have been largely failures, that these humans were very persistent—
ignoring repeated failures in pursuit of an idea and a belief that it
could be done.

This earliest known invention, if we consider how it could have
come about, raises a unique question concerning the evolution of the
human. The evolution of intellectual, cognitive, or creative capacities
followed different rules than those governing the evolution of other
abilities. A genetic alteration that produced wings useful for flying
only benefited those animals that shared that genetic characteristic.
To the extent that being able to fly provided an adaptational advantage, such a species prospered and grew. If any of the species did not
develop useful wings, they would not have survived as well. To be
useful, each individual animal had to possess the characteristic.

The same principles hold, of course, for humans also. The anatomical changes that occurred in the human hand, for example, that permitted finer manipulation and control had to exist in each individual
for it to benefit that individual. And, of course, all modern humans
possess such hands, capable of fine control and dexterity. There are,
certainly, individual differences—some humans are clumsier than
others—but the differences are small.

Abilities such as inventiveness, ingenuity, or creativity are different, however. All the humans that lived about two and a half million
years ago need not have had the idea of manufacturing tools with
sharp edges. Indeed, all of them need not have possessed the capacity to have such an idea or been able to accumulate the knowledge
necessary to make the idea workable. If one individual, or a small
group of them, invent a new process, others can, and do, imitate and
learn. Even with modern man invention and innovation are the products of very few persons, but the benefits of these products can be,
and are, shared by many. In short, everyone need not possess that

characteristic for it to benefit, and provide an adaptational advantage to, the entire species. We then have a paradoxical situation from an evolutionary point of view. Precisely those capacities that gave the species its major survival advantages were not directly connected with survival for each individual. As a result they could have been, probably were, and certainly still are, abilities which are sparsely represented in the population. In this kind of realm Lamarckian transmission holds: things learned by one generation are transmitted to the next.

What, exactly, were the advantages provided to an animal that could, at will, produce objects with sharp edges and sharp points? The answer to this question is, of course, not obscure; with these tools they could cut through the hides of animals to get the meat; they could dig, chop, and scrape; they could cut and make sharp points on wood. In short, at a minimum, they could more effectively exploit the food supply available in their immediate environment. At a maximum they could use these tools to manufacture other useful things. They could make carrying containers from the bark of trees or from animal skins, erect at least partial shelters and windbreaks, and do a variety of other possible things which we may imagine but about which we have no evidence. Once the tools existed, their use was only limited by the creativity, ingenuity, and imagination of the humans that possessed them.

By about one and a half million years ago one finds in Olduvai Gorge in East Africa (Leaky 1958) a marked change in the sophistication of the technology and in the variety of the stone tools that were manufactured. Given the label of "Acheulian" by archaeologists, these styles of tools, with minor variations in variety or prominence of one or another type, are found wherever humans are found for the following million or so years. They represent the prevalent, characteristic stone tool kit within which there was little change or improvement until about 300,000 to 200,000 years ago, an astonishingly long period for a technological plateau. Such stability, if one wants to call it that, cries for explanation and understanding. Why did it endure for so long, and what then happened that ended the long plateau? Of course, the first inclination is to examine what other things were or were not happening during this period, biologically and technologically. As we will see, a lot was changing indeed.

For one thing, the same physical species of human did not persist, or survive, through this entire period. By one and a half million years ago there lived, among other species of humans, one which had a larger cranial capacity, about 600 to perhaps 750 cubic centimeters. Looking backward, of course, the tendency has been to regard the species with the larger cranial capacity as being more important in the evolution of the human, and that species is the first to be called "Homo" by archaeologists. Whatever the realities of what were the exact evolutionary lines leading to modern man, it is clear that very marked evolutionary biological changes were taking place. By about one million years ago all the previous species of humans seem to have disappeared, replaced by one called "Homo erectus" with a brain size of about 1,000 cubic centimeters, and with hands much more closely resembling that of modern man.

No one, of course, wants to make much of sheer size of the brain. Such figures are quoted again and again because skulls have been found, and cranial capacity in cubic centimeters can be measured. Neural organization leaves few fossil traces (although Holloway (1974) does attempt to make inferences about it). Basically, everyone assumes that with the changes in size there were also changes in neural organization—that the brain was becoming more effective—an assumption that is not implausible viewed in relation to the clear dependence of this physically handicapped species on the products of the brain to survive and prosper.

It comes as a surprise, then, that throughout all this evolutionary development the stone tool industry changed little or not at all. To communicate some information about this state of affairs over this incredibly long period of time, without going into enormous detail about the stone tools found in various places, it is useful to quote some of the experts. Jelinek, in reviewing this long period of time, summarizes the state of affairs as follows:

> The overriding impression of the technological evidence in the archeological record is one of almost unimaginable monotony. Perhaps the most overwhelming example of this is the Acheulian of Olduvai Gorge, where for approximately a million years no significant innovation is discernible. (1977:28)

The site of Olduvai Gorge is particularly instructive because it contains fossils and artifacts spanning the period from about 1.8 million to about 400,000 years ago. Thus, there is frequently no equivocation whatsoever about temporal sequence—one layer lying directly above another layer must be more recent in time. The tools that are found in layer after layer, are largely the same in style, technique, and variety. There are even instances, during the period starting about 1.5 million years ago, of tools from older periods that are more skillfully made than tools from later times. Whatever small innovations did occur from time to time did not cumulate. Overall, Jelinek's use of the word "monotony" is appropriate.

This phenomenon is not, of course, restricted to Olduvai—it is general, and it persists well past the period that Olduvai represents so well. Discussing somewhat more recent times Butzer says:

> Overall, Acheulian toolkits from 500,000 to 200,000 B.P. [before present] may include some items that are more refined than any dating from 1.5 to 0.5 million B.P.; yet, in any one area, a range of sites spanning a few hundred thousand years will as often as not show a deterioration rather than an improvement in artifactual skills. (1977:579)

Obviously, there is an interesting question of why there was a technological plateau of such long duration: How can we explain it? And what does it imply about the human animal? One attempt to answer these questions is proposed by Butzer:

> This can be best explained by small population groups (of 20 to 50 people?) that included only one or two competent stoneworkers and that were widely dispersed in space. A single group might not encounter another group for as much as a generation. Thus, if the best stone craftsman was prematurely killed in a hunting accident, the stoneknapping skills of the group would be diminished for several generations or more. (1977:579)

But this kind of answer to the question is not at all satisfactory. First of all, one must remember that sometime around 1.5 million years ago there was a marked and highly significant technological innovation that spread throughout the human species of the time. Wynn (1979) makes the nature and magnitude of that change very clear. To manufacture tools of the older kind (2 million to 1.5 million years ago) the stoneworker could have relied, to some extent, on trial and error. The main requirement of producing a sharp edge with that technology was to remove flakes in pairs. "Even choppers with ten or eleven flake removals can be made simply by removing each flake in relation to one previous flake" (pp. 388–89).

The later Acheulian tools that were regularly patterned, symmetrical bifaces, however, could not be manufactured in such a simple manner. The stoneworker had to have a prior view of the end result to be achieved, and each flake had to be removed in relation to this overall prior view. As we have said, this big innovation spread widely— and no one imagines that before 1.5 million years ago, groups of humans were larger or less spatially dispersed. So the type of explanation summarized by Butzer cannot be accepted.

Jelinek offers a very different kind of explanation: "The repetition of patterns and lack of innovation suggest that they may have been the product of complex forms of imitative behavior . . . and that verbal direction played a minimal role in the learning processes associated with tool manufacture" (1977:15).

Jelinek is suggesting something which, if valid, is highly important. The level of development of language may not have been adequate for communicating about more sophisticated technology than that represented by the Acheulian. If this was the case, there would have been difficulty transmitting an innovation from generation to generation or from group to group. The limitation of relatively inadequate language might even have been more profound. One can imagine a human who has an idea for a new tool or a new technique but who cannot find the way to execute the idea. With an adequate language, the idea itself could be disseminated and, over several generations, a way to execute it might be invented. If the language was not adequate for the communication of the idea itself, the innovation might never materialize.

The issue of human language—how it arose, how it developed, and the level of its development at various stages of human evolution— remains an issue about which we can only speculate. Certainly, later on, language played such a massive role in the spread and accumulation of knowledge and technology that Jelinek's hypothesis has a ring of plausibility. The undetermined level of linguistic development may have been the cause of the prolonged plateau in stone tool technology.

So far, however, we have presented a very narrow look at human activity during this long period, so narrow as to be distorting. Stone artifacts so dominate the archaeological record that they also tend to dominate our thinking about early humans. To achieve a broader understanding of these humans, we must realize that the long plateau was confined to stone tools—in other areas there was certainly no plateau at all. On the contrary there was vigorous development along a variety of other lines.

By about one million years ago, when Homo erectus was the extant human, a remarkable phenomenon occurred, a phenomenon unique in the animal world. Humans began to move out of and away from their natural habitat and were able to live successfully in alien ecological conditions. Their fossil remains and their stone tools dating to that time have been found in Java, in North Africa, in parts of Southwest Asia. They even strayed as far away as southern France, where in the cave of Vallonet (de Lumley 1975) a few typical Acheulian stone choppers were found, dated to between 900,000 and 800,000 years ago. By about 500,000 years ago humans had spread pretty well all over Africa, Asia, and Europe—even living in latitudes far enough north to indicate that they were able to successfully cope with quite cold climates.

It is unimaginable that all this took place while technology was totally stagnant. As humans slowly, gradually, moved into areas with different temperatures, different rainfall patterns, different plant and animal species, different land terrains, they must have already invented ways effectively to cope with and exploit the conditions in these new areas.

The human species called Homo erectus lived for about seven or eight hundred thousand years, until 200,000 to 100,000 years ago— quite a long time for such a complex species to survive. They were, clearly, very successful animals. Major innovations, representing the realization of completely novel ideas, occurred during this period. Along with, and facilitating the gradual departure from their natural habitat, they invented ways to control their environment, to produce an artificial, man-made world, a momentous new direction for human ingenuity. About a half million years ago, possibly earlier, new conceptions arose, were communicated and spread, about how these humans could interact with their environment. They did not have to limit themselves to finding ways to cope with and to exploit the world in which they lived. They could also find ways to control and change their immediate environment. In other words, this animal realized that he need not always adapt to existing conditions—he could alter those conditions so that they suited him better.

For a long time humans had been discovering and inventing ways in which to exploit their environment more effectively. There are many (for example, Binford 1968), who interpret the fossil animal bone evidence as indicating that very early humans obtained meat more by scavenging than by hunting. There is little question, however, that by 500,000 years ago they were proficient hunters, killing and trapping game both large and small. It is also plausible to imagine that they increased the variety of plant food they used and the efficiency with which they gathered such food, although fossil remains of plant food are almost nonexistent from such long times ago. They probably had devised means of manufacturing containers for carrying things. They had undoubtedly invented a variety of uses for the skins of the animals they killed. We know, factually, nothing about how they used wood and what they may have manufactured from wood with the aid of their sharp-edged stone tools. But we must assume that they did use wood—we are talking about a highly developed, very ingenious species.

There is an essential difference, however, between exploiting the environment and controlling or changing it. Let us take fire as an example to illustrate the nature of the difference. All animals encountered and experienced the consequences of fire. Fires occurred naturally in a variety of circumstances, and the consequences were frequently frightening and catastrophic. About all any animal could do about it was to move, as rapidly as possible, away from the fire to a place that, hopefully, the flames would not reach. It may not have been difficult to discover and learn that fires did not invade rocky, totally barren areas or large extents of water. Rains that occurred probably also taught them something about the deterrent effect of water on fire. And one can be sure that humans invented ways to protect themselves, more or less adequately, from these unwanted natural events.

But some humans did more than this. Some humans conceived the idea, perhaps while some fire was dying out, that if they could control the fire they could use its heat to their advantage; if they could save and control fire, they could accomplish an amazing thing—they could change the local climate; they could make it locally warm even when the general condition was cold.

This conception, more or less well-defined, had to exist in the human mind before they were able to succeed in controlling fire. Consider that in order to invent ways to control this hazardous phenomenon, a great deal of close observation and exploration had to take place. And consider, also, that early attempts to use fire may well have been rather disastrous. The prior conception, and conviction about it, had to sustain the persistence and outweigh the failures. Once fire was effectively saved and controlled, the human had, in his possession, a powerful, new tool for controlling, not simply exploiting, aspects of his immediate environment.

All this occurred a long time ago. At Choukutien, in northern China, there is clear evidence of the extensive use of fire, presumably to create warmth in a very cold climate, evidence that dates back to between 500,000 and 400,000 years ago. At a site called Terra Amata, now situated in the modern city of Nice on the Mediterranean coast of France, dated to somewhere between 400,000 and 300,000 years ago, there are the ash-filled remains of several hearths that these humans used for their fires. They even knew enough to protect those hearths from drafts. A small wall of stones or pebbles was built up, always on the northeast side of the hearth, the direction of the prevailing wind (de Lumley 1975). These are, of course, not the only places showing evidence of the use of fire. There are many more from those periods of time. Clearly, all technology was not stagnant; new discoveries and conceptions continued to be communicated and spread.

Fire was not the only way that humans had devised to control their environment that far back in the past. They had also figured out a way to make it calm, locally, when it was too windy, and to make it dry, locally, when it was raining—they built covered shelters. One of the best examples is also located at Terra Amata where post-holes clearly indicate the existence of an oval-shaped, rather large, structure. The angles of the post-holes show that the poles were set in the ground all inclining toward the center. Covering this skeletal framework with branches and with animal hides could have provided good temporary shelter from inclement conditions.

Someone may feel inclined to protest—why call this controlling the environment? Why does the building of a shelter indicate anything more than protecting oneself against the environment? But there is a difference between taking advantage of natural shelter and constructing one's own artificial shelter wherever and whenever one chooses. In the latter case, by means of building, the human created shelter where none existed naturally and by doing this, altered the environment. And by virtue of this ability to change the local world, humans could live in places that provided no natural shelter. Everywhere they went there was potential shelter that they could construct.

The human had begun to develop an extensive technology. There must have been more inventions than we know about or even guess about, since our guesses tend to be limited by the knowledge of what practices continued into later periods. The precise state to which Homo erectus pushed technology is, however, much less important than the fact of the initial innovation. Together with his new conception of the possible relationship between himself and the environment, the departure of man from his natural habitat was an event fully as important as the first manufacture of tools. It was also a cumulative event—without his tools, and his other discoveries and inventions, this departure would not have been possible. The technology invented by these humans enabled them to live anywhere they chose to live.

Another way to put it, of course, is that humans could not survive outside their natural habitat without their technology. And from this time on the human became more and more dependent on technology in order to survive. The human, tied irrevocably to his technology, no longer had a natural habitat—indeed, applied to modern man the entire concept of a natural habitat seems ridiculous.

A process had been started that was irreversible. The only biological changes that could significantly affect the ability of the human to survive continued to be changes related to creativity, ingenuity, inventiveness—changes that could produce a more powerful technology. The course of human evolution was increasingly predetermined by the humans themselves; human action had specified which biological changes would or would not be important.

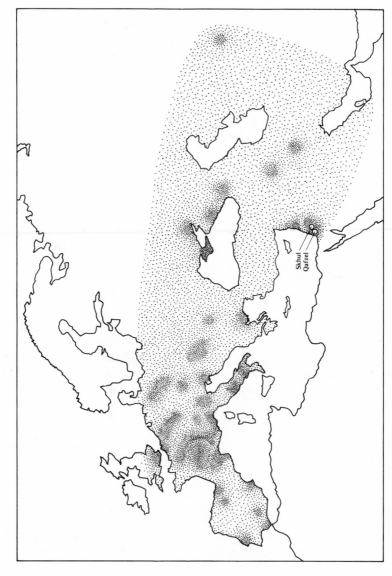

Map 2 Eurasian Distribution of Neanderthal Man. Areas in Europe and Western Asia inhabited by "Neanderthal" man. Skhul and Qafzeh may be the earliest known instances of Modern man.

CHAPTER THREE
Our Immediate Predecessors

B Y about 100,000 years ago the very successful human species, Homo erectus, had disappeared. A new species of human existed everywhere in the then inhabited world, a species long known as Neanderthal man in accord with the established archaeological practice of naming species after the place in which the first discovery was made, in this case the Neander Valley in what is now Germany. The transition from Homo erectus to the Neanderthals was not a sudden one—we need not imagine quick migrations, invasions, or exterminations. It was a very gradual transition that occurred over a period of about 200,000 years, or put differently, approximately 10,000 generations. Transitional fossil human crania have been found in western Asia, in southeastern Europe, and in Africa.

Neanderthal man has had, for many years, a very bad press, very bad public relations. The word, without capitals, has come to mean extremely out of date, uncouth, and brutish. The fault lies with the description of, and inferences about, the species by the original discoverer in the nineteenth century. The desire to set modern man apart, and on a pedestal, led to a conception of Neanderthal man as extraordinarily primitive, relying on brute force, his heavy brow ridges obviously indicating animal brutishness.

Only recently, in the last twenty years, has it become abundantly clear that they were very advanced humans. It is increasingly recognized that their abilities were relatively close to those of modern man. The newer terminology calls them "Homo sapiens neanderthalensis" but, not being bound by the traditions of archaeological nomenclature we will drop the last word in that phrase. We will call these humans simply "Homo sapiens" because it is also now well known that there was considerable morphological diversity among them in different parts of the world. Many skulls found in Africa and western Asia have quite different cranial characteristics from those in western Europe.

Homo sapiens had a skull with a cranial capacity as large or slightly larger than our own. The size and the thickness of the fossil bones and the evidence of muscle tendon insertions make it clear that Homo sapiens was stronger, more heavily muscled, than we are today. Of course, as we have said, brain size is not a necessary indication of neural organization and functioning, and greater strength and greater weight are not unequivocal advantages for any species, certainly not for humans. So we will not dwell on the physical characteristics of Homo sapiens but rather on the evidence of his behavior and accomplishments and on what these reveal about the directions of human evolution. First, however, we must orient ourselves to a new time scale because it is not only what was done but also how long it took to do it that is revealing. We started talking about humans in terms of the passage of one or two million years; then our time scale shrank and, with Homo erectus, we talked about hundreds of thousands of years. Now, with Homo sapiens, there is another order of magnitude of reduction in our time scale. We now must think about tens of thousands of years. The total span of existence of this species was remarkably short—only about 60,000 years. By 40,000 to 35,000 years ago Homo sapiens had, in turn, disappeared.

During this short period of 60,000 years these humans improved markedly on already invented technologies, introduced some new inventions, and began some social practices that had never before existed. The list is not endless but it is appreciable—from Homo erectus to Homo sapiens there was a considerable biological jump.

At least two significant innovations were introduced into stone tool technology by Homo sapiens to produce better tools more reliably and to produce different shapes of stone tools. One of these is the introduction of the "soft hammer." There were some advantages to be gained by striking a flint core with a "hammer" of antler or bone or even wood, rather than with another stone, to produce sharp-edged flakes. If used properly, the softer striking object permitted sharper angles of impact resulting in longer flakes and in somewhat better control of the flake production. Depending on the purpose, the objective, the nature, and function of the tool to be manufactured, then, different techniques could be and were employed.

Another and even more interesting invention involved core preparation. Instead of striking blades directly from the original block of, say, flint, the shape of the core is carefully pre-formed so as to determine the length and shape of the flake that will fall off. Using such techniques, flakes that are long and narrow, or broad and flat, or discoid in shape can be reliably and efficiently produced.

The techniques of core preparation are especially interesting because of what they imply about the conceptual abilities of Homo sapiens. To employ such a technique, to say nothing about inventing it, requires not only a clear, preconceived image of the end result to be achieved but also requires envisioning how to prepare the originally rather shapeless core so that the form of the final prespecified flake is assured. It seems highly unlikely that one could learn such technique by simply watching and imitating. For someone to learn to do this, the ultimate purpose would have to be explained at the very beginning and, even more, the relationship of the steps in core preparation to the distant, final objective would have to be understood. The spread and wide use of such techniques among Homo sapiens, is, perhaps, the best evidence for assuming that they possessed a more developed imagination and a language capable of communicating complicated ideas, images, and relationships.

Indeed, perhaps even more than this is implied. Even with the ability to communicate such things, how would a person who did not know the techniques learn them? Unless we imagine a prevalence of toolmakers, unable to work without appropriate vocalization, continually muttering aloud about what they are doing and why, the communication of complicated ideas implies active, intentional teaching. Such an interest in instructing others may have existed in previous species but, with Homo sapiens, its presence seems very likely.

It is interesting, as David Premack pointed out to me, that nonhuman primates do not engage in pedagogy—they do not intentionally instruct others. There are instances of innovation and discovery that occur in nonhuman primate groups and there are instances in which such innovation spreads to others in the group, but not as a result of teaching, only as a result of watching and imitating. For example, Menzel (1972) reports that one chimpanzee discovered how to use a pole as a vaulting instrument. Others, by watching, also learned it and soon the chimpanzees could not be kept in their cage. But in no instance was there any indication that one animal attempted to help another to learn.

Kawai (1965), in another example, reports on a group of monkeys in which two innovations occurred, one of which is rather remarkable. For experimental reasons grains of wheat were strewn on the sand as food for the monkeys. One of them invented a flotation method for separating the wheat from the sand. The mixture was thrown into the sea, the sand sinking and the wheat grains rising to the top. The wheat could then be gathered and eaten without sand. Some others learned to do this by watching but, again, there is no evidence of trying to teach. Apparently, only humans are compulsive pedagogues, and it is a good bet that this characteristic was strongly represented in Homo sapiens.

The stone tool industry associated with Homo sapiens is called Mousterian, following the same practice of naming a type after the first archaeological site at which it was identified. However, the so-called Mousterian varies widely; the common, linking factor is primarily the level of technological sophistication. As Bordes (1968) says about different sites in different places: "Although they often present striking marks of originality, they have this much in common, that they are at a certain technical and typological level which may be reached earlier or later according to the particular locality" (p. 98).

These artifacts are the collective expression of the cognitive and communicative abilities of Homo sapiens. To the extent that we are correct in supposing that language limitation was at least one major factor hampering the further technological development of Homo erectus, we must attribute a level of language to Homo sapiens that was adequate for the communication of ideas, purpose, and intentions. The considerable variability in the Mousterian tool collections also indicates that Homo sapiens was not content to adopt invention and innovation but also was creative enough to try new styles and find what suited a particular group best. The new technologies spread widely just as they had in the past but they were adapted to local preferences, not simply copied. Homo sapiens was considerably more creative and inventive, in effect, than was Homo erectus.

It would be surprising if we did not find clear evidence of other manifestations of the creativity and intellect of Homo sapiens, and these do exist in abundance. There are, however, some grave difficulties in pinning down, with certainty, all of the innovations and advances made by this new species.

For example, during the period in which Homo sapiens existed, perhaps dating to even earlier times, one finds some instances of the working of wood and the use of wood for a variety of purposes. In Saxony a wooden pointed spear with a fire-hardened tip was found dating to this period; worked wood, clearly used as tools, were found in Spain; wood sliced at a slant making a sharp edge, dating to about 60,000 years or more, comes from northern Rhodesia; a broken wooden spear with a sharpened point was found at Clacton, England;

large pieces of tree bark were found in northern Rhodesia in shapes, and in a context, strongly suggesting that the bark was used as a container or a carrying device (Bordes 1968).

The use of tree bark to manufacture containers, making wooden tools and wooden spears, and particularly the discovery that fire could be used to harden a wooden point are all major innovations. But wood does not preserve well at all. It is naturally rare that one finds wooden artifacts dating back to the period of Homo sapiens. One could hardly expect to find wooden tools still preserved dating back to, say, 300,000 years ago, even if such tools had existed then in profusion. So while we know from the excavations that Homo sapiens used wood for a variety of purposes, and while we may suspect that his use of wood was vastly greater and his wooden tools more precise than those of Homo erectus, we cannot be certain of this.

With regard to some of the other innovations we are more fortunate. Stone hearths and ashes do preserve reasonably well, and it is clear that Homo sapiens greatly expanded the extent of use of fire and, undoubtedly, the variety of purposes for which it was used. In addition to the already mentioned use of fire to harden a wooden tip, fire also was used for cooking. This, of course, represents an invention with major implications since it had the potentiality for enormously expanding the usable food supply. There is a large variety of both plant and animal food that can be made edible, or more easily edible, by the use of heat.

They were also clearly better hunters than Homo erectus. They successfully hunted everything: mammoth, wild bear, deer, aurochs, horse, gazelle, whatever there was. It is easy to underestimate the significant underlying achievements that this represents. To be a very successful hunter, in addition to adequate traps and hunting weapons, one needs an accumulation of knowledge. One must understand the habits and preferences, the strengths and weaknesses, of the animal in order to trap it or kill it. Such knowledge was being accumulated, and *transmitted* by Homo sapiens.

The inference is very strong, although the evidence is scanty, that Homo sapiens also were the first to begin the conquest of water. This had consequences which, at the time, were certainly unimaginable. For more than three million years water had been a danger to the human and also a barrier, limiting and constraining his movement. He could not cross a lake or a deep, wide river, nor could he venture outward from the seashore. We all know that eventually water was transformed into an asset, from being a barrier to movement it became a facilitator of movement. For many, many thousands of years transportation over water was much easier than transportation over land. Water, when it was conquered, also provided an abundant supply of food which had not previously been available.

The conquest of water must have been a considerable intellectual feat, taking many, many generations. It was certainly easy for even the earliest humans to observe that some objects floated on water—pieces of wood, leaves, and even some varieties of animals, ducks, for example. But such observations are no more useful for conquering water than watching birds fly is to the conquest of the air. The original idea must arise that a floating object may be able to support another object that, by itself, sinks. And even this is not enough. There exists the marvelous example of the Indians of Mesoamerica who knew about the wheel—they used it on toys—but never realized its possible utilitarian value. One had to discover that, say, a fallen tree trunk, afloat in the water, could support a human and, moreover, that the human could make the combination move and could direct its motion, steer it. And perhaps, then it would have been possible to proceed to the notion of building more stable rafts.

What is the evidence that suggests that Homo sapiens had reached such a point? One kind of evidence comes from a comparison of style of stone tools. There were clear stylistic differences between the stone tool industries of northern Africa, on the one hand, and western Asia on the other. The styles in France, Italy, and southeastern Europe were related to the styles in western Asia. The style in Spain, however, of the late Acheulian and the early Mousterian industries showed very clear affinities to the style of North Africa (Bordes 1968; Freeman 1975).

It seems then that Homo sapiens did not come to the Iberian peninsula through the Bosporus but, rather, directly from Africa across what is now the Strait of Gibraltar. If such crossings had occurred at the height of what is known as the Riis glaciation (the one preceding the very last glacial period) the water level would, of course, have been much lower. It is rather unlikely, however, that a dry land bridge would have existed. They would have had to cross a considerable body of water (Freeman 1975). I do not want to suggest, on the basis of this evidence, that Homo sapiens were far along on the path of conquering water. I do think it likely that they were on the path, however. Some have suggested that the earliest artifacts attributable to the presence of humans in Australia should be dated to between 60,000 and 50,000 years ago. If this is correct, it might suggest that some groups of Homo sapiens built rafts that, at least by inadvertence, could have traversed very large sea distances. This, however, is highly speculative at present.

Another possible indication of progress in the conquest of water might come from finding evidence of use of food from the sea. Although such use did not become extensive until much later, there are occasional finds that clearly date back to Homo sapiens. Klein (1975) reports that shellfish remains at the Klasies river mouth cave "dating to beyond 100,000 years ago, so far constitute the oldest evidence for regular exploitation of marine resources . . . although active fishing may have remained beyond the technological capabilities of the Klasies people" (p. 240). Wendorf and Schild (1980) report a concentration of remains of fish clearly indicating extensive fishing in a site in the western desert of Egypt dating back to about 40,000 years ago. They also mention similar concentrations of fish remains at the Georgian cave sight of Kudaro. Perhaps the best evidence comes from sites in Spain, clearly associated with Homo sapiens, in which oyster-shell and top-shell have been found. It is highly suggestive that these sites are situated so as to have easy access to both the sea and the mountains (Freeman 1973). Again, I think, the evidence points to Homo sapiens having started the gradual process of conquering water.

Perhaps of even greater importance than the technological developments are indications of changes in life styles and the emergence of belief systems in Homo sapiens that clearly establish a continuity with modern man. Humans, as we already know, had always lived in small-size groups, hunting animals and gathering plants for food. It was a mobile existence. If the food resources within reasonable distance of their camp dwindled, because of depletion or of seasonal changes, they moved and established another camp in an area where food was more plentiful. The major requirement for a campsite, other than food resources, was the reasonable availability of fresh water. How often they moved during a given year is not known. It undoubtedly depended on the richness of food supplies that year and on the size of the group. A large group would exhaust the food in an area more rapidly than would a smaller group. Because some excavated sites are small and seem to have been occupied for relatively short periods, while others are larger and were clearly repeatedly occupied, it seems likely that these human groups returned seasonally to a base camp.

With Homo sapiens we have evidence of at least occasional departures from such a pattern. The basis on which such an assertion can be made about behavior patterns at a time so long ago needs some explanation. Most animals, unlike humans, produce their young only within a rather restricted period of the year, one or two months. If an animal is killed within say, the first year of its life, it is possible to know how old that animal was at the time of death on the basis of the stage of development of teeth and some bones. If one knows how old the animal was, one also knows, as a consequence, the approximate time of the year in which it was killed.

Bordes and Sonneville-Bordes have this to say about the matter, discussing sites clearly occupied by Homo sapiens: In southwest France "the study of reindeer teeth and antlers shows that in many cases these animals were killed all the year round and thus that the shelters were occupied also all the year round, at least by part of the tribe. This does not preclude the possibility of hunting expeditions or temporary camps" (1970:65). Indeed, at least in that part of the world, these experts have the following view: "The semi-sedentary population would, at rather long intervals, move from one shelter to another inside a given territory, and, more rarely, change its territory" (pp. 72–73).

To call these groups "semi-sedentary" rather than "seasonally mobile" perhaps accurately reflects the change in life style introduced by Homo sapiens. Clearly, these humans were able to use their better hunting ability, the use of fire for cooking, and perhaps other means of exploiting their environment to reduce the frequency with which they had to move from one camp to another, in short, to establish partial permanence. In addition to the fact that they were able to do this one must emphasize the fact that they chose to do it.

There is another important characteristic, one which may be peculiarly human, which first appears with Homo sapiens. With this species one finds widespread, undeniable evidence of an aesthetic sense. There are some who think that aesthetic expression was in evidence long before Homo sapiens, but this is based on interpretations about the nonutilitarian aspects of some types of stone tools. It may or may not be a correct interpretation. Long before Homo sapiens appeared on the scene, humans had begun to manufacture tools that were regularly shaped with careful bilateral symmetry. Most experts agree that the careful shaping and the symmetry add little to the usefulness or efficiency of the object as a tool. Hence, as Bordes suggests, "we should perhaps see in it the first tentative expression of the aesthetic sense" (1968:137). Certainly, these symmetrical tools are more pleasing to the "eye" of today's human, but reasoning backward like that to the "eye" of humans a million years ago is problematic. And perhaps they saw uses for these forms that we do not imagine. It must remain merely suggestive.

More direct testimony to the importance of aesthetics arrives when one finds evidence of the use of coloring material and artifacts that are unequivocally ornamental in purpose. There are no instances of ornaments before the time of Homo sapiens, and the possible earlier use of color for decoration is highly equivocal. Wreschner (1980), who has exhaustively searched through the evidence, cites three instances of finds of red coloring matter in layers or excavations associated with Homo erectus, one at Olduvai (Leakey 1958), one at Ambrona (Howell 1966), and another at Terra Amata (de Lumley and Boone 1976).

Butzer, however, disputes the aesthetic or sociocultural interpretations of these very early finds. Apart from the specific problems in each case, he makes the general point that the use of fire frequently leaves unintended red coloring and "the baked sediment can easily simulate ocher powder to the uninitiated" (1980:635).

Apart from having noted that the controversy exists, however, we will ignore it. Perhaps Homo sapiens carried on and further developed various aesthetically pleasing practices, or perhaps they were the first to have a clearly developed aesthetic sense. Whichever is the truth, it is clear that by 50,000 to 40,000 years ago the use of color, primarily red and black, for decoration is a frequent occurrence. In many sites from this period one finds numerous fragments of red or black coloring matter, and occasionally one even finds the instruments that were used for grinding the coloring matter into powder (see Bordes 1968:145–46). Dart and Beaumont (1971) even report the existence of an ocher-mining site in South Africa that is dated to about 42,000 years ago.

Perhaps even more convincing than the presence of coloring material are the finds of deliberately manufactured ornaments. These are not frequent, in fact they are rare for the period in which Homo sapiens lived, but they do exist and come from widely separated localities. From Tata, near Budapest, a site dated to about 50,000 years ago, comes an amulet, made from nummulite which is engraved with two crossing lines (Bordes 1968:110). From the same site comes an oval-shaped plaque, made from a section of a mammoth's molar tooth, carefully rounded and polished and showing evidence of once having been colored with red (reported in Marshack 1976).

Marshack (1976) also describes two ornamental pendants from La Quina in France, originally reported by Martin. One is made from a reindeer phalange and another from a fox canine tooth. Both have small holes drilled through them for hanging. Marshack has also diligently searched for, and describes, a number of artifacts deliberately inscribed with parallel lines, zigzags, or other forms, dating back to Homo sapiens. Although he wishes to interpret these as notational in some way, they could also have simply been decorative.

The evolution of an aesthetic sense in an animal is a curious phenomenon. Evolution is usually thought of as a process totally governed by adaptational and survival advantages. If a genetic change occurs that does not provide such an advantage, it does not persist. But it is difficult to imagine the survival advantages of an aesthetic sense, although some ingenious humans will be able, no doubt, to make such an argument. It is simpler, however, to realize that there may occur some genetic change in a very complicated animal that does produce a distinct biological advantage for survival but, as an irrelevant by-product, may also be accompanied by other characteristics that could have no bearing on survival. Such characteristics could persist even if, alone, they might have been slightly detrimental. The human aesthetic sense may have arisen in connection with changes that increased imagination and creativity, the total complex being inseparable.

One final behavior innovation of Homo sapiens remains to be discussed, a most curious new practice. Homo sapiens, from time to time, deliberately buried dead individuals. Before this species existed such a practice was, presumably, unknown—no evidence even suggestive of burial has ever been uncovered dating to more than 80,000 years ago.

What would have given rise to such a strange idea in the first place? Why would they have gone to the trouble of digging a large enough hole, putting the dead body in it, and covering it? What could conceivably have motivated and perpetuated such a practice? Obviously, since we do not know, and will not know, precisely what went on in the minds of Homo sapiens, we will have trouble answering such questions. Let us, however, assemble the few facts that exist about burials during this period.

Not everyone was buried; indeed it seemes likely that burial was only an occasional event. According to Phillips (1980) nearly 200 individuals are known from sites associated with Homo sapiens in Europe and the Near East, but Harrold (1980) finds only 36 instances that are clearly burials. And of these 36, 22 come from just four sites: Le Ferrassie in France, Shanidar in Iraq, and both Skhul and Qafzeh in Israel. There are many, many excavated sites in which no burials are found. Even if Harrold, insisting on clear evidence for including the case as a burial, has discarded too many instances, the incidence of burial is clearly small. And if buried skeletons, better protected from animal scavengers and the eroding effects of climate, are more likely to have lasted all these years, then the proportion of burials may have been very small indeed.

There is enormous variation in the form of different burials. There is at least one instance of deliberate decapitation; some bodies are buried in extended position while some are so tightly flexed that they were probably bound before burial; others are in moderately flexed positions—in short, all kinds of burial positions are found. Some bodies were buried together with artifacts such as stone tools while others were not. The only regularity that Harrold (1980) could find among his 36 cases was a marked tendency for male burials, and not female burials, to be accompanied by "grave goods."

And these things are about all we know. Needless to say, many things have been said and written about burial practices. It is very common to encounter a phrase such as "cult of the dead." Such a phrase, however, denotes nothing in addition to the facts of burial, although it connotes some evocation of magic. Some believe that burials, particularly when they involve skeletons in strongly flexed positions or when the buried body is covered with heavy stones, represent an attempt to prevent the dead from rising again (e.g., Maringer 1960). Others frequently take the presence of "grave goods" to indicate a belief in a continued existence for the dead, one in which they would have need for the implements, implying concern for the well-being of these dead individuals (e.g., James 1957:22–23).

None of these statements represent things we know. They are speculations, and while I do not object to speculations, it is preferable if the speculations are grounded, at least partially, in the scanty data that do exist. The source for most speculations about the meaning of burial practices, however, is not the data from the past but rather knowledge of the belief systems concerning death that currently exist in various groups. They represent extrapolations backward in time from current beliefs and practices about dead individuals found in Western societies or in contemporary simpler, "primitive" groups. But contemporary beliefs, be they found in complex or in simple societies, have gone through at least 50,000 more years of trial, change, and alteration. Extrapolation backward in time, all by itself, is unlikely to be fruitful.

We will leave the matter for now as a mystery. We will return to it in a later chapter in which we will be dealing with periods from which there is more evidence. The practice of burial not only continued but became very widespread and, curiously, more variable from place to place. Not too many thousands of years later there are clear connections between burial and religious practice, connections that may or may not have existed for Homo sapiens.

Homo sapiens, as a species, disappeared between 40,000 and 35,000 years ago. There is much unclarity and controversy in the literature about the evolutionary continuity between Homo sapiens and the new species that supplanted them. But from this chapter it is clear that there can be no question as to the cultural continuities. The new biological species is the modern human, the human that exists today. And here we encounter one of the rare but spectacular instances of the failure of human imagination and creativity: this modern human is officially called Homo sapiens sapiens. It may represent a dangerous trend. In the scientific literature, for example, there is a species of animal that is officially called "gorilla gorilla gorilla." I am, fortunately, not bound by official terminology and will simply call the currently extant human species "Modern man."

CHAPTER FOUR
The Transition to Modern Man

Someday soon, with luck, much more will be known about the replacement of Homo sapiens by the new species of human that still exists today. While the transition from Homo erectus to Homo sapiens can be traced over a period of about 200,000 years, most experts believe that only about 5,000 years elapsed between Homo sapiens and Homo sapiens sapiens—Modern man.

That short period of time, 5,000 years, creates a problem for those concerned with the biological evolution of the modern human; 5,000 years does not seem long enough by far, a mere 250 generations or so is a laughably small number. So there was, until relatively recently, a temptation to think of Modern man evolving in some distant, unknown place, then migrating to and invading the areas inhabited by Homo sapiens, destroying that species.

But such ideas must be discarded—there is no support for them in the data. Nowhere is there any evidence of populations or large groups of Homo sapiens having met a violent end. It is true, as Trinkaus (1978) points out, that many Homo sapiens fossil remains show evidence of injury, but it is abundantly clear that these represent the results of accidents during life or, more frequently, damage to the skeletal remains after death.

A major part of the problem of understanding this transition to Modern man lay in the original description of Homo sapiens, Neanderthal man, as he was called, that was widely accepted as designating the species. The image, as we have seen, was of a massive, rather mindless, ugly brute vastly different from the sensitive and sapient humans that uncovered that specimen. Such could not conceivably have been a close progenitor of Modern man but, of necessity, had to be seen as an accidental bywater in the evolution of the human. But Homo sapiens was, in truth, not so distant from early Modern man, not technologically and, in some parts of the world, not even very different in the shape of the skull. Western Asia, rather than Europe, provides a better picture of the physical diversities present among different groups of Homo sapiens and, perhaps, makes the transition to Homo sapiens sapiens seem like less of a mystery.

There have been skulls and skeletons from that period uncovered in western Asia that are close, in their physical dimensions and characteristics, to the western European Homo sapiens. Examples of these are the crania from Shanidar Cave in the Zagros dating to about 45,000 years ago (Solecki 1959) and the skull excavated in Tabun Cave in the Carmel hills which is, perhaps, 50,000 to 60,000 years old (Garrod and Bate 1937). Such similarities should surprise no one— human groups spread widely. But until relatively recently insufficient notice has been taken of human fossil skulls from the same general area, dating back to the same periods of time, that do not resemble those of western European Homo sapiens.

In Skhul Cave, also in the Carmel region, several skulls were uncovered that date to between 50,000 and 45,000 years ago (Howells 1975). One of these, known as Skhul IV, seems intermediate between western European Homo sapiens and Modern man on a variety of skull measurements. Skhul V is even closer to, and almost indistinguishable from, many fossil skulls that are clearly Modern man.

Even more impressive are the finds from the grotto of Qafzeh in the Galilee, near Nazareth (Vandermeersch 1978). Remains of six adults and of ten children have been found dating back to the period with which we are concerned. The two best preserved and most complete crania have been analyzed in detail. Qafzeh 9 and Qafzeh 6, as these skulls are known, are indistinguishable from those of Modern man. There is much debate about the exact dating of the Qafzeh remains. On the basis of similarities in microvertebrate fossil remains with those of more securely dated sites, together with geological similarities traceable to events that affected the entire calcerous zone of the Central Levant, Bar-Yosef and Vandermeersch (1981) are inclined to date the occupation of Qafzeh to about 80,000 years ago, very early indeed. Others disagree, citing amino-acid dating of some of the human bones that indicate somewhere between 40,000 and 45,000 years ago, although there is general acknowledgment that such dating is not very reliable. Jelinek (personal communication) also argues on the basis of ingenious analysis of the characteristics of the stone tools, that the true dates for Qafzeh will turn out to be about 40,000 years ago. It is possible, then, that the transition from Homo sapiens to Modern man occurred over a period of 40,000 years or so rather than only 5,000 years.

Whatever the answer to these questions turns out to be, another point must be made about the transition: there is clear cultural continuity between Homo sapiens and Homo sapiens sapiens. The ways of living did not change abruptly; the innovations of Homo sapiens were continued and accelerated and, of course, there were some new inventions. Many are fond of thinking of the advent of Modern man as the beginning of a sudden spurt of development—technological, cultural, and social. But if we look at the known evidence carefully, this is simply not true. The picture is primarily one of a continuation of prior practices; changes occurred but they were gradual in their pattern. Perhaps, there was some reduction of the time scale, some quickening of events, but not of a magnitude that is easily discernible. In the period from 40,000 to 20,000 years ago there are relatively few things that hit the eye.

The major techniques of working stone remained the same; the different styles that appeared did not necessarily represent successively better tools. Bone points do make their appearance about 30,000 years ago, both in Europe (Phillips 1980:72; Klein 1973) and in western Asia (Bar-Yosef 1980:117), but they were rather rare. Bone tools gradually increased in frequency and variety, but it is not until about 15,000 years ago that they represented an important part of the tool kit of human groups.

There is some evidence that medium distance trade may have been developing as long as 30,000 to 25,000 years ago. The presence of sea shells in many localities that are far from the sea (e.g., Hahn 1972) and the frequent existence, in small quantities, of varieties of flint that were not locally available (e.g., Kozlowsky 1972–73) seem to indicate importations from places that are sometimes as far away as 400 kilometers. These instances do not unequivocally demonstrate organized trade, however. Such importations could have occurred during seasonal migrations of groups: movements over such distances were probably not unusual. After all, 250 kilometers could easily be covered in a week of not strenuous walking. But the beginnings of trade and barter are at least equally plausible interpretations, and the evidence for trade increases gradually as the millennia unfold.

Of great interest is the evidence that between 25,000 and 20,000 years ago, there was the beginning of construction that was intended to have some durability. Temporary construction, of course, had been around for a very long time. But now one begins to see the very beginnings of a different concept in construction. Bosinski (1969, referred to by Phillips 1980) reports a site near the Rhine River in which there had been two tents, temporary structures, but also a pavement of stones covering the 3-meter area between the tents. Kozlowski and Kubiak (1972) found the remains of three structures that must have represented an attempt to achieve durability. They were constructed almost entirely of mammoth bones, the structure built not with the customary post holes, but on a solid foundation of other mammoth bones. Perhaps most indicative of this early trend is the report by Phillips (1980:95) that at a campsite in southern Germany there was found a stone wall that was almost a meter in height. The instances are rare, but the beginnings existed.

This picture of continuity and slow, gradual development does not apply to one aspect of human behavior. Although there is evidence, as shown in the previous chapter, that Homo sapiens used color for decoration and did manufacture some ornaments, the vast explosion of such activities with the advent of Modern man is sudden and remarkable. Amulets, pendants, earrings, and pierced decorative seashells suddenly are found almost everywhere, and in profusion. Stone, bone, wood, antlers, and ivory are all carefully worked for decorative purposes. And, perhaps, we can infer something about the importance of decoration to these people from the fact that, in many instances, the ornamental seashells had to be brought from very far away.

Not only does one find this proliferation of decoration, but a totally new dimension also appears in the realm of aesthetics—incised, painted, and sculpted figures of animals and of humans. The cave paintings from France and Spain, many of them magnificent, are the most well known. I will not try to do them justice here, either descriptively or interpretatively—they have been described and pictured by many experts. There is also much that has been written about the meaning of these cave paintings. Some see religion, some see magic, some see repositories of knowledge, some see sexual and conceptual symbolism. The fact is that one can interpret them in any way that an ingenious mind would like to. There are almost no constraints on such interpretations. Perhaps the task is as difficult as it would be to interpret and ascribe functional meaning to a random collection of Picasso paintings, while having very little knowledge of the culture and concerns and ways of life of the times in which they were produced.

We do know that Modern man did produce such painting and drawing almost from the very beginning of his appearance in western Europe. The oldest of the cave paintings probably date back to about 30,000 years ago. While some are mediocre, many were painted by persons of magnificent artistic talent. Nothing resembling such activity existed prior to Modern man. Another thing we know is rather curious. Many of the paintings on the walls of the caves were in places where natural light, direct or reflected, could not reach in sufficient intensity to either enable the human to do the painting or to enable anyone to view it. We will not speculate here about why those artists chose to do this. But they clearly must have been able to produce usable light from torches or lamps.

Another astonishing fact is that this practice, rather pervasive in that region, did not spread widely. It remained primarily confined to portions of France and Spain. But other forms of artistic expression were widespread. Carvings of animals and of human figures, the latter usually exaggerated or stylized, and incised drawings on stone, bone, and mammoth ivory are found all over western and eastern Europe, the oldest dating back at least 30,000 years. It is only later that similar drawings and figurines appear in western Asia and elsewhere. Again, some are crude and others were clearly made by very talented humans. Again, there is no indication of any such activity prior to Modern man.

One must come to the conclusion that the biological differences between Homo sapiens and Homo sapiens sapiens did not primarily involve ingenuity and inventiveness. The narrow path of evolution had broadened. The primary differences that are revealed in the archaeological record concern decoration, aesthetics, and the representation of things in the world in drawings, paintings, and sculpture. This is where we find the explosion after the advent of Modern man. The comparable explosion in the products of inventiveness and ingenuity, namely technology, does not occur until much later, starting perhaps only 11,000 or 12,000 years ago in western Asia—nearly 30,000 years after Modern man had replaced Homo sapiens.

I cannot help but wonder again about any conceivable adaptational, reproductive, or survival advantage that might be conferred on an animal who colors and decorates and makes images from reality and from imagination. Of course, some of the characteristics of an inventive animal are also relevant for aesthetic expression: imagination, creativity, and curiosity are necessarily integral in both processes. So I continue to believe that the aesthetic sense, perhaps aesthetic need, that we see first in Homo sapiens and see explosively in Modern man represents an evolutionary peculiarity. Characteristics that happened to develop coincidentally to other advantageous changes did not disappear; indeed they developed further, even though, in and of themselves, they were "useless." And as we know, it was not, and is not, a trivial characteristic.

It would be hard to exaggerate the importance of aesthetics to these humans and the time and effort expended in such activities even in instances where the products clearly are unrelated to any plausible symbolism or meaning. The very number of decorative and ornamental artifacts indicates the large amount of time spent in these pursuits. In addition, utilitarian objects came to be manufactured so that they, too, were aesthetically pleasing. Many of the stone tools, for example, were carefully worked so that they not only had sharp edges and points but pleasing symmetrical shapes. One of the most persuasive instances illustrating this can be seen with the much later invention of pottery, an extremely useful invention. It is remarkable that around the time of its appearance there is no appreciable period whatsoever in which one finds undecorated pottery. Almost from its very inception, pottery was decorated: the aesthetic need was always there.

As one might expect from a creature as ingenious as the human, aesthetic activity did not remain nonutilitarian forever. Uses were discovered for what had once been simply decorative or image making. At some point humans realized that a drawing of a sheep, for example, could be used to store and communicate information. So, if one person sold three sheep to another, three drawings of sheep together with some identifying mark could form a record of the transaction. Thus, by 5,500 years ago one finds such proto-writing, the predecessor of a true system of written language, in Mesopotamia, in Egypt, and in other places.

It is conceivable, as Marshack (1976) believes, that the idea and practice of using images or marks to store and communicate information goes back much further in time—30,000 years or more. It is true that many pieces of bone or stone or antler have been uncovered that have lines and marks of all kinds inscribed on them: parallel lines, crossing lines, zigzag lines, meandering lines, V-shaped marks, circular indentations, all kinds of things. There is no way to know whether or not these had meaning as information to those who made them. They could just as well have represented attempts to produce pleasing patterns, idle doodles, or whatever. The likelihood seems low, however, that they had information value. Any system of recording information, no matter how primitive, would have had something systematic about it. Otherwise, the person recording the information could hardly intend for it to be retrievable later on, even by himself. And there is nothing systematic, nothing repetitive about these early markings.

If it took 30,000 years to invent the idea of permanent information storage, easily retrievable and communicable, we should not be surprised—rather we should be impressed. It was truly a novel idea, the implications and consequences of which certainly could not have been foreseen. Eventually, it revolutionized the human way of life and continues to do so.

The remaining chapters of this book are about the last 15,000 years of the existence of Modern man. In those millennia the pace of change truly accelerates—soon a minuscule amount of time, say 500 years, begins to make a big difference. The changes, of course, are not biological—they are social, psychological, and technological changes.

In spite of the fact that there is at least a 25,000-year lag between the advent of Modern man, a new biological species, and the onset of this period of ever-accelerating change, there is a temptation to attribute it all to biological characteristics of the new species. There is also, perhaps, an egotistical and slightly arrogant desire to see ourselves, Modern man, as hugely different—better, of course—from Homo sapiens. We cannot know whether or not, if the species Homo sapiens had continued to exist and modern man had never evolved, the accumulation of knowledge and technology would have led to a similar development.

It seems possible that Modern man was a better "accumulator" of knowledge than Homo sapiens. If he were, then one could accept the 25,000-year lag between the appearance of the new species and the technological spurt as a period in which the necessary knowledge grew and grew until it made new endeavors possible. There are two possible senses in which Modern man might have been better able to accumulate knowledge, one psychobiological, the other social. Modern man may have emerged with a neural organization that produced more effective memory and better mechanisms for information processing. Modern man may also, by developing language to a higher level, have been able to communicate better, and hence, accumulate knowledge on a group basis more adequately.

Needless to say, there has been considerable speculation about both of these questions. The issue of neural organization has been dealt with by Holloway (1974), who has attempted to infer details of brain structure, and hence neural organization, from fossil cranial markings. These efforts, however, remain rather inconclusive. Jerison (1973), with the same issue in mind, has been led to the idea that because of "modular" neural organization, brain size in relation to body size does accurately reflect the "intelligence" of a species. But if this viewpoint is correct, then Homo sapiens was the intellectual equal of Modern man. His cranial capacity was not less than ours. The question is left unresolved.

On the issue of spoken language, a serious attempt has been made by Lieberman (1975) to say something about its evolution and about possible differences between Homo sapiens and Modern Man. Through his analysis of how human speech sounds are produced, he demonstrates that the "right-angle bend is the crucial anatomical feature" (p. 115) of the two-tube vocal tract that enables adult Modern man to produce the full range of vowels and consonants. The chimpanzee and the newborn human infant, for example, do not have such a structure and are, consequently, highly limited in the sounds they can produce. Particularly important for communication by means of spoken language, according to Lieberman's analysis, is the fact that without such a right-angled two-tube vocal tract, the animal is unable to produce the most stable vowel sounds; that is, those vowels which are most easily distinguished from others and retain that distinguishability even with small departures from the ideal position of tongue and vocal tract are the ones that the chimpanzee cannot utter. Thus, if any of the human species that existed before Modern man did not have the two-tubed system, there would have been limitations on spoken language.

Lieberman and Crelin (1971) come to the conclusion that Homo sapiens was not able to produce the full range of human speech sounds. While there is little or no disagreement about the first part of Lieberman's analysis, there is considerable disagreement as to the correctness of the assertion about Homo sapiens. Le May (1975) and Burr (1976) argue strongly and persuasively that Homo sapiens probably could produce the same range of sounds as Modern man.

Perhaps, anyway, the question is unanswerable by such an approach, regardless of who is correct about the vocal tract of Homo sapiens. Speech and language, as a system of communication, require much more and, at the same time, much less than the production of a certain set of sounds. As Lieberman (1975) himself points out, language requires the neural organization to code and decode speech sounds, to code and decode syntactical organization, and also involves considerable cognitive ability. The consequences of not being able to produce the entire range of possible human speech sounds might be minimal and trivial. One does not need the entire array of sounds, and there exists no language today in which all the possible sounds are used. Some, as for example Japanese, use very few sounds indeed.

If a species that used spoken language was incapable of producing a number of the stable vowel sounds, this could easily be compensated for by introducing more redundancy into speech and having longer words. Thus, the only consequence might be to slow down information exchange somewhat. Alternatively, the basic units of speech could be different with more emphasis on pitch, pauses, and the duration of sounds. As George Miller pointed out to me once, even a system as impoverished, as lacking in variety of sounds, as the Morse Code presents no insuperable barrier to communication by means of spoken language.

So we cannot say with certainty, today, what the differences were between Homo sapiens and Modern man, nor can we say anything about the magnitude of differences that may have existed. Differences did exist, however, that must have had significance for survival. By 35,000 years ago Homo sapiens is no more. Everywhere one looks there are only varieties of Modern man.

We, then, are the most recent, the currently extant but certainly not final, version of humans. We have evolved as an animal that is creative, ingenious, inventive, and bent on controlling his environment. This animal is also imaginative, artistic, compulsively pedagogic, and social. At least these characteristics seem plausible to infer from the paleontological and archaeological record as we know it today. There are, undoubtedly, other innate characteristics of this highly complex animal that we have no hint of from what we know about the distant, evolutionary, past.

We may, however, be able to learn more by looking at the more recent past. What has Modern man done with his abilities and inclinations? How did we come to our current behavior patterns, complex societies, and intricate belief systems?

PART TWO
THE MARCH TO "CIVILIZATION"

CHAPTER FIVE
Toward Sedentary Living

A SEASONALLY mobile pattern of existence has a lot to recommend it. To imagine what it might have been like about twenty thousand years ago, do not think of a straggly band of humans, half-undernourished, forced to keep moving from camp to camp in their search for food. Perhaps such an image might be appropriate for much earlier human species in very bad years, but it no longer applied to the existence of Homo sapiens and certainly not to the life style of Modern man. As we may recall, Homo sapiens in southwest France had already become so effective in exploiting the food resources in that environment that Bordes and Sonneville-Bordes (1970) talk about them as a "semi-sedentary population." They did not have to change camp frequently.

To picture the existence of Modern man, think rather of a well-fed group who spent part of the year, spring and summer perhaps, in one place and the rest of the year in another. Each of their camps, one of which may have been more "permanent" than the other, would have been chosen to be in the midst of plentiful food supplies and for ease of living in the climate of the appropriate season. True, it would have been somewhat of a burden to pack up belongings, walk for two or three days (or perhaps even weeks) to the new site, and to erect the temporary shelters and facilities needed by the group. But, by doing this twice a year, perhaps sometimes three times a year, they could have the best of all possible worlds, easy and pleasant living conditions without excessively hard work.

Perhaps this picture is overdrawn a bit; perhaps even Modern man, at an early stage like 30,000 years ago, had to move more often in bad years, and perhaps highly desirable campsite locations were not always reachable or available. By 15,000 years ago, however, it is probably not overdrawn. With Modern man, the expansion of the potential food supply continued, perhaps even more rapidly than before. About 20,000 years ago, two major new food sources started to become very important. Food from the sea and from lakes, fish and sea shells, which had previously only been available in small, sporadic, quantities began to appear as major items of the human diet. In addition, on the basis of the prevalence of mortars in the Near East, one can infer the appreciable use of cereal grains, a food source which assumed more and more importance as time went on. Considering population densities and the state of technological development, these new food sources, in addition to the foods relied on previously, presented a plentiful supply most times in most of the areas of the world in which humans lived.

Human population was not very large and the inhabited areas were sparsely peopled. A seasonally mobile way of life was not difficult and presented all the advantages I have described, advantages great enough to induce people today, who can afford it, to turn again to such a way of life, in quite different circumstances, of course. Some people I know live in New York in the spring and fall, in Florida in the winter, and on the Cape or the Vinyard in the summer.

Nevertheless, about 11,000 years ago, one finds clear evidence of communities that did not change locations: they remained in one place all year long. The "hows" and "whys" of this change which, once started, gradually swept the entire inhabited world, represent fascinating questions that have been hotly debated. Let us examine the facts of the matter and the possible interpretations by looking at the situation in that part of the world where sedentary, year-round occupation of the same site first made its appearance, namely, the Levant, particularly in the areas that are now Israel and Lebanon.

It seems parodoxical that the change from seasonally mobile to sedentary existence first occurred in a part of the world in which a mobile existence was very easy. The point is that in this area there are great changes in climate as one moves over comparatively short distances, either east–west or north–south. A little bit of climatic geography will help to understand this. There is today a narrow coastal plain bordering the Mediterranean, running roughly north to south the entire length of the region, a plain that is rarely more than 10 kilometers wide. This coastal plain enjoys a typical Mediterranean climate. Fifteen thousand years ago, before the melting of the glaciers and ice sheets that covered many other parts of the world, the water level everywhere was, of course, much lower. The levantine coastal plain at that time was wider by another 10 to 20 kilometers. It is a small digression, but it should be pointed out that human groups undoubtedly lived on that wider coastal plain and that, unfortunately, those living sites which existed in the area now under water are totally unknown to us. The only sites we know about are ones that are now on dry land.

If one travels eastward from the coastal plain, one climbs rapidly into hills. In a mere 30 to 50 kilometers one is in a rather different climate, 500 to 600 meters above sea level. The winter at this altitude is very rainy, considerably colder than the Mediterranean coast, and quite humid. The summers are sunny and dry, hot days and cool nights. If one continues to travel eastward, there is a precipitous drop into the Jordan Rift valley and still another climate. In a distance of, perhaps, 35 kilometers one finds oneself about 400 meters below sea level in a hot, dry, desert climate. The changes that one finds in the north–south direction, although less sudden and precipitous, are equally pronounced. In the south are the Sinai and Negev deserts. The farther north one travels, the rainier it gets. Over a distance of 400 kilometers one moves from harsh, dry desert to fertile country.

Some 15,000 years ago this whole area was probably somewhat cooler and drier than it is today, but the sharp climatic differences existed then as well. The different climate areas, of course, supported different plants and animals and were optimally hospitable for humans at different times of the year. Wild wheat and barley, for example, flourished best in the hills; ibex lived well in rocky, semi-arid regions; wild goats and many varieties of deer were more prevalent to the north in Lebanon; gazelles were plentiful in the Jordan valley and on the fringes of the deserts. The distances that a seasonally mobile group of humans would have to travel to locate their camp in an auspicious area for a given time of the year would not have been large at all. This is the basis for the assertion that in that part of the world, a seasonally mobile, hunter and gatherer style of existence was quite tenable, posing few if any difficulties.

Let us continue, then, by trying to picture, as well as we can, the activities of the human groups that lived in this area in the period from about 17,000 B.C. to 10,000 B.C., the time span identified by archaeologists as corresponding to one or another of the Kebaran technological and cultural complexes. It is the last clearly designatable culture in the Levant before we begin to see evidence of a change in life style toward sedentary existence. Bar-Yosef (1982) has presented an excellent account of this period, including data from sites that have still not been adequately published. We can do no better than to follow his account.

As we might expect from seasonally mobile humans who lived by hunting and gathering, the number of people in a group that lived and moved together is quite small during this entire period of six or seven millennia. The size of such a group has to be inferred, of course, from the size of the sites that have been discovered and there is, of course, considerable variability—not all campsites cover the same extent. A site that was returned to again and again would be larger while some very temporary hunting camp might be confined to a quite small area of only 25 to 50 square meters. Bar-Yosef has examined the reports on about 30 sites dating to between 17,000 B.C. and 12,500 B.C., together with about 35 later sites covering the period up to about 11,000 B.C.; this later period, with a slightly different style of stone tool, is referred to as "Geometric Kebaran." His conclusion is that the largest of these Kebaran living groups contained, perhaps, "four nuclear families." He characterizes this as a cautious estimate, but even if one does not want to be cautious, the group size is small.

Where they chose to live is, naturally, an easier inference to make. The larger sites, 450 square meters at most, are exclusively in lowland areas, either in the Mediterranean climate of the coastal plain or in the Jordan valley, with a predilection for the former. These larger, lowland sites probably represent the base camps that were occupied for the major part of the year and were returned to every year. The sites in the inland hilly areas are smaller and were probably seasonal summer camps. Such was the distribution of campsites for the entire Levant, with no differences between the early and later Kebaran periods, except for the most southern areas. No Kebaran sites at all have been found south of the Beer Sheva valley dating to before 12,500 B.C., in other words, the most arid regions were unoccupied during this drier period of climate. A period of climatic amelioration with higher humidity enabled human groups to move into the Negev, and even into the Sinai, deserts in the later "Geometric Kebaran" period. None of these desert campsites were large: the maximum found is about 150 square meters in area. These desert sites probably represent more temporary wintertime locations.

The Kebaran was not a particularly innovative period. The stone tool industry was, of course, highly developed with its roots in the preceding millennia. Very few bone tools are found in Kebaran sites and the ones that do exist are in the pattern of the preceding 10,000 years. Ground stone implements, bowls, mortars, pestles, tools for grinding and for pounding, do exist but they are very few in number.

It is generally assumed that in addition to pounding red ocher these tools were used to pound or grind roasted wild cereal grains that were part of the diet. The sites where these tools have been found were, however, located in areas in which conditions for the preservation of plant remains were poor and, so, direct evidence for the use of cereal grains does not exist. The animal bones uncovered indicate clearly that they hunted and ate whichever ungulates were most available in the general area of the camp. Remains of birds are scanty, an occasional pigeon or buzzard or goose.

The picture is reasonably clear and consistent. These people had evolved a rather stable mode of existence in which small groups probably lived quite well, moving once or twice a year. The area was not densely populated, and the food supply was undoubtedly quite adequate most of the time. For six to seven thousand years this same technical and cultural complex persisted; stability is the dominant theme. The size of group did not change; except for the desert areas the preferences in location of campsites remained the same; the same basic tools, with small variations and minor stylistic differences, continued throughout the period. To the archaeologist, a Kebaran campsite is easily and immediately recognizable; they were so similar for so many thousands of years that they became, as Bar-Yosef says, somewhat boring.

And then, suddenly, there was a change—suddenly meaning within several hundred years. The Natufian techno-cultural complex that replaced the Kebaran in that part of the world lasted a relatively short time, as these things go, from about 10,500 to 8,500 B.C. For some reason, a pattern of life that had been stable for quite a few thousand years yielded to new and different influences. Whether those new influences arose through contacts with distant groups or were entirely indigenous is not known, but it is clear that the results were many and varied. Since sedentary existence, the year-round occupation of the same site, began with the Natufians, a detailed examination of the beginning of this phenomenon may illuminate how this radical change in life style came about, a change that had momentous implications for the future of human groups.

First of all it is necessary to stress that the Natufians were still hunters of wild game and gatherers of wild plant food. In some few locations fishing also supplied an appreciable part of their available food. There is no suggestion in any of the evidence from the Natufian sites that plant food production or animal husbandry, that is, agriculture, had begun. This is important to emphasize because it is not so long ago that specialists almost uniformly held that agriculture preceded, was a necessary precondition, for humans to be able to settle down in one place. Flannery ably characterizes this previously dominant view: "Once agriculture had freed man from the eternal food quest he was able to give up his ceaseless wandering and settle in villages where he perfected pottery making, loom weaving, and all the hallmarks of sedentary life" (1972:23). And he goes on to comment that: "Archeological discoveries over the last ten years have not been kind to this reconstruction. From the Near East came the discovery of fully sedentary communities dating to 8,000 B.C., yet lacking all evidence of domesticated animals or phenotypically domestic cereals" (p. 23).

We now know that in the Near East sedentary existence preceded agriculture by quite a stretch of time and a different understanding of the sequence of developments is needed. Let us begin our examination by looking at the evidence for the earliest sedentary sites. While most of the Natufian sites were still within the same size range as the Kebaran sites, there are a few that are considerably larger, more than 1,000 square meters. It is among these that the evidence exists for year-round occupation, evidence which, taken as a whole, is reasonably compelling.

One of the things that is taken as an indication that a site may have been occupied all year round is the presence of well-constructed, durable houses. Perrot, who excavated 'Eynan, a village in eastern Galilee, was one of the first to point this out at a time when most still believed that a permanent settlement could not exist without agriculture. At 'Eynan, dated to about 9,500 B.C., he found the remains of stone houses, probably roofed with reeds, that he estimates housed a community of about 150 people. Such construction represents considerable time and effort, and the main argument is that such permanent dwellings would not have been built by groups that were seasonally mobile. Perrot says:

> The existence at 'Eynan of a permanent settlement with true houses is a new and important fact, not so much the building of houses itself . . . as the permanence of the settlement before a stage of food production had been reached. . . . At a time when Natufian hunters roaming the Lower Jordan Valley were visiting the Jericho spring and oasis, 'Eynan, in exceptionally favorable conditions, was already a permanent settlement. (1963:21–22)

Another example can be taken from Mureybit, a village in Syria dating to about 8,500 B.C. Van Loon, the excavator, cautiously says:

> The finds do, however, suggest that a permanent settlement of perhaps as many as 200 one family houses existed here for at least four centuries. . . . The ancient inhabitants of Mureybit seem to have subsisted by hunting and the gathering of wild plants alone. (1968:280)

The existence of houses durably constructed would not be, all by itself, totally convincing evidence of sedentary existence. One could argue, and some have, that it merely indicates that the inhabitants spent enough time there during each year to make the construction worth the time and effort. But other evidence does exist to strengthen the conclusion that these larger villages were occupied all year round. Cauvin (1978) carefully examined the potential of the immediate environments to sustain year-round existence, given the technology and food-use patterns of the Natufians. He also inquired whether or not the distribution of debris, artifacts, and fossils makes the assertion of year-round residence reasonable. He comes to the conclusion that three places, Mureybit, Abu Hureira and 'Eynan were, indeed, sedentary settlements.

And there is still a third piece of evidence, perhaps the most convincing of all, that is mentioned by Bar-Yosef (1982). He points out that these locations contain "abundant remains of human commensals such as the house-mouse, the rat, and the sparrow. These two rodents and the sparrow constitute the dominant percentage of rodents and birds at Hayonim cave, indicating that occupation of the cave and, almost certainly, the terrace was a year round phenomenon" (ms., p. 26).

Thus, before 9,000 B.C., for the first time in human prehistory, some groups in western Asia settled to live in one place all through the year, not as an occasional, exceptional event in a very good year, but permanently, year after year. Why did they do this? There is, of course, a strong temptation to say that humans had probably been trying to settle down for hundreds of thousands of years, perhaps millions, and that they did so as soon as they were able to. After all, we know that they succeeded in reducing the number of movements they had to make each year; we know that even 50,000 years ago there were occasions on which some humans succeeded in remaining in one place for a whole year. Clearly, it had been going on for a long time, and why not. Why would humans not rid themselves of the burdens of a mobile existence for an easier, more comfortable, sedentary life? Who wants to be always on the move?

Perhaps this is a correct view. It is certainly an easy view to take. The trouble is, though, that not all humans showed this eagerness to settle down. At the time of the Natufian culture many, undoubtedly most, groups continued their seasonally mobile existence. Thousands of years later, when sedentary existence was more nearly the norm, there were still many groups who did not settle down to live in one place. Even today there are small groups here and there, pushed into the least habitable places, who continue a mobile existence of one kind or another. They are even known to vigorously resist pressures to settle down.

The human is a complex animal. He likes security and also likes adventure; he likes comfort but frequently chooses to endure rigors. Perhaps the safest thing to say is that a sedentary existence seemed to present enough advantages so that if it became possible, there were many who chose it. It was a step, though, that also had unfortunate consequences and was irreversible and self-perpetuating, as we shall see.

At this point, however, let us examine what made it possible for some Natufian groups to settle down, something that the Kebarans had not been able to do, assuming they would have wanted it or resisted it equally. The surprising thing is that in the Natufian techno-cultural complex we do not see what one might expect: there is not a large array of innovations, new inventions, and new foods which might have made settled existence easier to accomplish. There are rather a host of small changes, no single one of them amounting to too much.

The flaked stone tool industry does not show any remarkable changes from the Kebaran to the Natufian cultures. Indeed, the Natufian flint tools may be somewhat less skillfully made than in the Kebaran period. There are only two innovations: bone-hafted sickle blades with a characteristic sheen on the edges indicating that they were used to cut grasses, and elongated flint picks, the use of which is uncertain. These only appear in Natufian sites. Backed flint blades with sheen on the edges do appear in Kebaran sites but not the hafted sickles. The rest of the flaked stone tool industry is not very different from the Kebaran.

There are many changes from the Kebaran to the Natufian in other

kinds of tools but, again, these changes do not represent new invention as much as they represent different emphasis and extent of use.
While tools made from animal bones and ground stone tools for
pounding and grinding are found in Kebaran sites, they are relatively
rare. They were not used intensively. Natufian sites, in contrast, yield
rich collections of bone tools, tools for hunting, fishing, and hide
working, and in addition a considerable amount of jewelry made from
bone. Similarly, pounding and grinding tools are found everywhere
in profusion in Natufian sites, their number and variety far exceeding
earlier cultures. In all of this heavy reliance on bone and ground stone
tools there are not many new inventions, only the greater use of ones
already known for thousands of years.

Indeed, there is only one completely new kind of tool, but this may
have been an important one. The Natufians introduced tools for
straightening wooden shafts. These tools were simple in conception
and consisted of a deep parallel-sided groove ground, usually, into
basalt stone. Shafts were straightened in the deep groove after the
stone was heated, producing a significant difference in the quality of
arrow shafts, which would certainly have improved hunting effectiveness.

Although it can hardly be expected to explain the ability of some
Natufian groups to settle into year-round residence in the same place,
there was also a considerable increase in the quality and variety of
jewelry and ornaments. Ornaments, necklaces, bracelets, and figurines were made from various kinds of stone, from bones, from teeth,
and from a large variety of marine mollusks. There are some indications from the materials used that the Natufians probably traded more
extensively than the preceding Kebaran people.

What does all this amount to in trying to understand how the Natufians were able, here and there, to adopt a sedentary life style. How
were they able to get enough food in all seasons of the year in one
place? The answer to this question should be easy, reasonable, and
very plausible if we imagine that some groups chose to settle down
because it seemed to offer, in many ways, an easier life. In the absence of a good answer we might have to think of the possibility that
some set of circumstances or pressures forced them to stop moving
seasonally and, as a consequence, they had to do as well as they
could in one place.

No one big change enabled sedentary existence: the evidence points
clearly to an accumulation of many small things. The Natufians be-

came better, more effective, hunters than their predecessors. In addition to straighter arrow shafts and the possibility that these arrows were bone-pointed, there is another important fact that we have not yet mentioned. They had domesticated the dog (Davis and Valla 1978) which, if used for hunting, would have been a considerable asset, especially for animals such as gazelles, who can be herded and run with the help of dogs. The animal bone remains in Natufian sites indicates that gazelles were a major source of meat.

There is the possibility, and some believe it important, that the Natufians were better able to exploit food sources from the sea. Bone fishhooks are found at numerous Natufian sites and this, obviously, strengthens the possibility. On the other hand, there is a paucity of direct supporting evidence. Few, if any, shellfish remains are found in Natufian sites, and with the exception of the sedentary village of 'Eynan, fishbone remains are rather scarce. At 'Eynan things were different. Situated near the shore of a large lake, the fossil evidence indicates heavy reliance on fish—perhaps more even than on meat. It seems sensible to conclude that while aquatic resources may have been effectively exploited here and there, it was not generally important in understanding the Natufian departures from mobile existence.

Probably the most important dietary change that enabled sedentary existence to be sustained was the sharply increased reliance on cereal grains by the Natufian people. The evidence for this is strong, consisting of three independent indications. First, there is the widespread appearance of the bone-hafted sickle blades that were clearly used to cut cereal grasses. Second, there is the great increase in pounding tools, tools that would have been needed to pound and grind the grain. The third point is even more direct. Fossil teeth found in almost all Natufian sites exhibit marked signs of attrition and dental caries, symptoms that Smith (1972) unequivocally associates with considerable consumption of cereal grain.

The importance of such heavy reliance on cereal grains for sustaining a sedentary existence needs and deserves some explanation. No matter how benign and well situated a geographic location is, there will be periods of the year when food resources at that place are scarce. If one is to live in one place all year round, one either submits to periodic hardship and hunger or one finds ways to store and preserve food in seasons of plenty for use during seasons of scarcity. Cereal grains such as wheat and barley were plentiful and easily gathered in the proper season—they grew wild in dense stands all over the hills of that area—and what is more important, dried cereal grains are eminently storable. Provided they are kept dry, they do not deteriorate. Cereal grains represented a food that could easily tide groups over the lean parts of the year. It is amusing, as an aside, to realize that occasional storage failures were not always totally negative in their impact. It was undoubtedly instances of stored barley getting slightly moist that led to the discovery of beer.

There is one other change from the Kebaran to the Natufian that is of significance, a change in where they chose to locate their camps. While many Kebaran sites were located on the coastal plain, this is not true of Natufian sites. These latter sites are generally located within the hilly areas or on the flanks of the hills near wadi outlets. The point is that they chose locations near the interstices of different ecological zones. Thus, from the same site there was access to animals and plants that thrived in the plains and to different varieties in the hills.

Thus, an accumulation of little things made a major change in life style possible: more effective hunting, the domestication of the dog, the increased consumption of fish here and there, the greater reliance on storable cereal grains, the more judicious choice of living sites and what Bar-Yosef describes as the "intensified use of previously invented technologies" (1980:125). All these things added up; they added up to the ability in some places to stay put, not to move as seasons changed. Some chose to do this even though it had a cost to it. To store cereal grains, one had to build storage bins that could be kept dry. Increased reliance on cereal grains meant the considerable labor of threshing, roasting, and grinding. It is not clear that even in its simplest form such a sedentary existence offered marked advantages in convenience in comparison to moving one's camp once or twice a year.

So we must remind ourselves, and it is not surprising, that not all Natufian groups chose this new way of life. Many did not. In this general region of the world different choices of life style still are made by different groups when options are available. For example, in the Zagros mountain areas that lie above 1,000 meters, although most of the villages are occupied throughout the year, "Two of the tribes are still migratory, leaving their summer camps in the high country . . . with the onset of cold weather and trekking down into the lower valleys or piedmont for the winter season" (Braidwood and Howe

1960:17). But those who did choose the sedentary style of life, those who established communities in which they lived all year round, profoundly affected the future.

It has been frequently been said that the beginning of food production, of agriculture, was the monumental revolution in human groups. But it seems to me, and I will try to explain why in ensuing chapters, that the fundamental change was from seasonally mobile to sedentary existence. For many reasons this change could not be undone and led inevitably onward. There is an old saying that "coming events cast their shadows before." But, in Natufian times there were no shadows of what was to come. Perhaps the saying does not include periods of time like two or three thousand years.

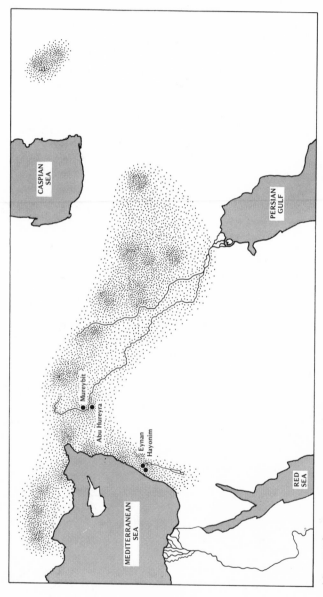

Map 3 The Levant and the Jordan Valley. Early Sedentary Villages. The black circles represent some of the earliest nonagricultural sedentary villages. Shaded areas indicate the general location of early farming villages.

CHAPTER SIX

The Size of Sedentary Groups

WHATEVER the advantages and disadvantages that may have been expected to follow from the change to sedentary existence, at least one major consequence could not then have been known. We now know that abandonment of a mobile life style in favor of living in one place all year round has been uniformly accompanied by sizable increases in population. Why this occurs, how inevitable it is, and how we can tell that it did occur 11,000 years ago are questions that need to be answered.

During the more than three million years of seasonal movement the size of the human group that lived together, and moved together, remained rather small. The exact size is, of course, not easily determined and there are disagreements about this. But whether the groups consisted of nuclear families, eight to fifteen individuals, or whether at certain times and places the group size approached numbers like fifty, is not an important issue for us. We can think of that entire range as rather small. When, however, as we noted in the preceding chapter, we find rather clear evidence of sedentary existence in some of the Natufian sites about 11,000 years ago, we find much larger groups for the first time: those permanent sites housed about 150 or more persons by reasonable estimates.

To reemphasize the point, we can compare the size of living sites in the same geographic area, namely the Levant, before and during the Natufian era. Bar-Yosef (1982) gives an excellent summary of these data. For the Kebaran period, lasting from about 17,000 B.C. to 12,500 B.C., the sites range (not counting very small camps of 15 to 25 square meters) from 100 to 150 square meters (e.g., Ein Gev 1) to areas not larger than 350 to 400 square meters (e.g., Kebarah Cave, and Kefar Darom 8). These are all small areas: the largest would correspond to a circle with a diameter of about 20 meters. Considering that part of such areas were used as working spaces and as dumps, the number of men, women, and children certainly could not have exceeded, say, forty. In the period called Geometric Kebaran (the style of the stone projectile points had changed), dating from 12,500 B.C.

to about 11,000 B.C., the size of the sites was unchanged. The largest (e.g., Hefsibah) is again not greater than 400 square meters.

During the Natufian period, lasting from about 10,500 B.C. to 8,500 B.C., the same general pattern continues: predominantly the Natufian camps were about the same size and, presumably, contained about the same number of people. One still finds some small sites of, perhaps, 100 square meters, and one finds many that are between 400 and 500 square meters in area. This range includes the vast majority of the Natufian sites. There are, however, a few exceptions, no more than six in number, that are all more than 1,000 square meters in size, more than double that of the largest of the usual campsite. These large sites are also precisely the ones that indicate extensive construction activities and show other indications of sedentary existence. These are the places where humans first succeeded in establishing reliable, permanent, year-round residence. The coincidence between sedentary existence and larger group size is unmistakable.

There are really only two possible answers to the question of why these sedentary sites are so much larger than the others. One answer is that, for some reason, smaller groups that had had periodic contact with one another while they lived in a mobile life style agglomerated—perhaps at the site that had been their usual meeting place. The other possible answer is that with sedentary existence dramatic local increases in population took place and necessitated enlarging the size of the settlement.

The first of these possible answers, agglomeration of several smaller groups, is attractive and simple but, if examined closely, does not seem plausible. Let us briefly recapitulate our line of reasoning concerning the events that led up to sedentary existence. The attractions that a less mobile life style held for humans were not new: they date back at least to Homo sapiens and, probably, to long before them. Humans tried to reduce, more and more, the number of times they had to move each year—indeed this is one of the factors that kept group size small, since a larger group would exhaust the food supplies in a given location more quickly. Eventually, by a combination of more effective hunting, a more diversified food supply, and increased use of foods that could easily be stored for long periods of time, some groups found locations in which they could live all year round and chose to do so.

A location that could support sedentary existence for a group of 40 or 50, however, would not necessarily be able to support such an existence for a group of 150. An agglomeration of separate groups in one location would have quickly defeated the attempt at year-round occupation. Such agglomerations might have occurred temporarily during a season of the year when food was particularly plentiful at that location, but such seasonal coming together of various groups would not have warranted the considerable work of building permanent dwellings for all. Certainly, the number of permanent dwellings are an indication of the number of permanent residents, estimated to be in the neighborhood of 150 men, women, and children in these early settled communities.

If we reject the agglomeration explanation, we are left with the alternative of believing that there was a relatively rapid local population increase approximately coincident in time with the beginning of sedentary existence. We cannot, however, just leave it at that since on the face of it, such a coincidence of population growth and sedentary life seems even less plausible than the answer we have just rejected. If the explanation of population increase is to be accepted, there must be more than coincidence involved: there must be a causal connection between the two phenomena. And if these two are causally connected, the direction of that causality is unequivocal—the population increase could never have facilitated sedentary existence. We are then left with the question of whether sedentary existence could plausibly have caused sudden population increase? The answer is that not only could it have done so but that rapid population increase would have been almost inevitable—unforeseen, unanticipated—but inevitable.

First, let us specify the dimensions of the problem: what do we mean when we speak of rapid population increase in these early sedentary Natufian communities. We are not talking about an increase in birth rate or longevity that might be called a "population explosion." It would not have been of a magnitude comparable, say, to current birth rates in Mexico or Pakistan, which imply a doubling of the population in thirty to thirty-five years. What we may conceive of, in those settlements of 10,000 or 11,000 years ago, is something like a tripling of the local population in the course of about two hundred years. We do not have to assume or to imagine sharp, drastic culture and behavior changes to explain this magnitude of population increase. Indeed, two things alone could be responsible. First, the fact that seasonally mobile women would have had a higher incidence of miscarriage and, second, the physiological factors that would have decreased the spacing between live births for sedentary groups.

The higher incidence of miscarriage during periods in which the group moved its camp from one place to another is a virtual certainty, although it is difficult to estimate the magnitude of the effect. Data on the frequency of miscarriage are very meager, even for modern societies. Henin (1969) reports a study from which we can, perhaps, get some rough clues. In analyzing fertility patterns among the Kawaha tribe in the Sudan, he compares one segment that ceased being nomadic in the 1920s, another that became sedentary in the 1950s, and a third part of the tribe that remained nomadic. In the two settled segments of the tribe he reports slightly fewer than 50 miscarriages per 1,000 pregnancies. Those who are still nomadic, however, are estimated to have almost 80 miscarriages per 1,000 pregnancies—a rather appreciable difference. We cannot take such numbers, however, as literally applying to the humans who lived 10,000 years ago. In the modern tribes there are also appreciable differences in adequacy of diet and ease of existence between the settled and nomadic groups. In addition, a modern nomadic life style is quite different from, and based on, other economic considerations than the life style of ancient seasonally mobile humans. It is probably reasonable to say, however, that at least some of the higher incidence of miscarriage results from the mobility of the group in and of itself.

The longer spacing between a woman's live births would have had a much larger effect. The reason to expect an effect of sedentary existence on birth spacing, however, requires some explanation. There exists, in the human female, a normal period of infertility following the birth of a child. The biochemical and physiological mechanisms responsible for this period of postpartum infertility are by no means clearly understood, but some of the factors affecting its duration are clear. The period of infertility is directly linked to the period of lactation and breast-feeding; the longer breast-feeding continues, the longer is ovulation delayed. It was originally believed that lactation itself was solely responsible for the effect but, as evidence accumulates, it seems that this is not entirely true. What emerges as the more critical factor in delaying ovulation is the duration of vigorous infant sucking at the mother's breast (Lee 1979). It is a curious, but biologically adaptive, phenomenon. As long as one child continues to depend solely, or primarily, on the mother's milk, the mother is unlikely to become pregnant again. Apart from the possible problem of sufficient milk for two children, it was biologically adaptive because of another obviously huge problem that existed for migratory groups if there were too many children (more than one per woman?) that had to be carried.

In modern agricultural and industrial societies these issues are almost insignificant. Frequently, bottle-feeding takes the place of the breast at a relatively early period and supplementary solid foods are also introduced—the period of postpartum infertility is brief. The humans who lived more than 10,000 years ago, however, had not yet domesticated animals (except for the dog) and had no alternative supply of milk available. Breast-feeding would have been the only food for the infant for, perhaps two years and the primary source of food for another year or so. We can then envision a natural customary spacing of three to four years between successive live births. With such spacing between children, an occasional miscarriage, and with, probably, no more than 50 percent of the children surviving to maturity, we can understand that the population of the time did not increase very rapidly.

We have not yet, however, addressed the question of why sedentary existence would have changed anything at all about this state of affairs. The key thing is the easier availability to sedentary groups of adequate supplementary foods for the infant. Assuming that these people did not have the techniques available to make and store purees of fruits and vegetables, the major kind of food that could be used early on for supplements to breast-feeding would have been ground and cooked cereal grain. Groups that stayed in one place all year round relied heavily on such grains, gathering and storing them in season. They, thus, would have had a year-round abundant source of supplementary food for the infant. Total weaning from the breast may or may not have occurred earlier for sedentary than for mobile groups but, with better supplementary foods, the infant would have fed less at the mother's breast, the result being a shortening of the period of postpartum infertility. The consequent reduction of the spacing between consecutive live births, perhaps to 2.5 or 3 years, would have produced a sizable, local population expansion for the sedentary group.

There are, of course, also a number of cultural and psychological factors that might have contributed to population increase with the change from mobile to sedentary living. Such factors would all center around the fact that without the necessity for moving the camp once or twice per year, it became less important to maintain wide spacing between successive births. Thus, if to any extent, mobile groups purposely fostered longer live-birth spacing by infanticide or by postpartum taboos on intercourse, such practices would have gradually diminished or disappeared. We have no way, however, of inferring anything about such possible birth control practices—the fact that they are found to exist in some contemporary groups tells us little about the past except to inform us that such practices are possible in human groups. This whole area of possible cultural and psychological influences on population 10,000 years ago must remain in the realm of unconstrained speculation.

So little is known about the factors affecting fertility and fecundity in humans, however, that one would like to substantiate all this by more than biological argument. We will, hence, resort to evidence from contemporary humans, extrapolating backward in time. Using observations about humans living today to establish something about humans who lived more than ten thousand years ago is, as we remind ourselves again and again, a procedure about which we must be wary. Biologically, they are undoubtedly the same, or near enough to make no difference, but very little of the behavior of humans is solely determined by biological processes. Behavior is almost always affected by psychological, social, and cultural factors also. And it is nonsense to imagine that any humans living today are the same, culturally, as those so far back in the past. No matter how simple the societal organization, the ways of living, or how "primitive" their belief systems may seem to us, one cannot regard any contemporary human group as indicative of how it was back then. There has, after all, been another ten thousand years or so of trying one thing or another, of thought and experience, of evolving cultural and belief systems that seem to work for the group. The only thing one can learn from such contemporary groups is that the way they live is one possible way in which a human group can live—not that it is in fact the way they did live long ago. So, in our use of evidence from contemporary humans we will try to stay as close as possible to the biological, otherwise we end up being able to say little with any real confidence.

There are numerous studies comparing birth rates in mobile and sedentary groups and, more importantly, there are some that describe the effects of the change from a mobile to a sedentary style of life. They all, without fail, indicate a markedly higher birth rate for the sedentary groups. Most of these studies, however, are of limited value for us. For example, Schaefer documents the large and sudden jump in the Eskimo birth rate that accompanied their incorporation into large, sedentary settlements: "the increase from less than 40 births per 1,000 in the mid-1950s to 64 per 1,000 ten years later" (1971:16). But it is difficult to know just to what to attribute this change. These Eskimos had been moved into permanent settlements with government subsidy and the provision of foods never before available to them. Removing them from their traditional sources of food forced a change in their total way of living. Although Schaefer wants to attribute the increased birth rate, in large measure, to the introduction of bottle feeding and the consequent reduced period of maternal lactation, many nutritional, psychological, and cultural changes were also going on simultaneously.

Perhaps the most carefully detailed study of the effects of a change from nomadic to a sedentary life style is presented by Lee (1979), who visited and studied the !Kung bushmen in the Kalahari desert of South Africa over a number of years. During the period from 1963 to 1973 the entire population was gradually changing in the direction of a more sedentary existence. During this rather short period of time appreciable changes in birth spacing were already apparent. Sharp differences exist when comparing the first half with the last half of the decade and, within each of these periods of time, between those women whose existence was more sedentary and those who were more nomadic. The largest difference can be seen by combining both of these factors: the more nomadic women in the period from 1963 to 1968 had, on the average, a period of 42 months between births while the more sedentary women in the period from 1968 to 1973 had an average interval of only 30 months.

In the short period of time encompassed by Lee's study, it cannot be that well-established cultural traditions, such as duration of taboos on sexual intercourse, had changed: such traditions have a life of their own. Lee (1979:325–30) presents an excellent, quite persuasive argument, supported by data, that links the change to, precisely, the easier availability of supplementary foods for the infant as the groups become sedentary.

The appearance of large sites for the first time in the entire history of human groups is, then, attributable to sedentary existence itself. The settlements would have had to expand as, over the generations, the population increased. Furthermore, the increase in population would not have seemed sudden or dramatic to the inhabitants of the settlement, another one or two houses to add every ten years or so.

Such a process would not have been a temporary, brief phenomenon and, of course, it was not. The sedentary sites that have been found, dating to the period between 8,500 B.C. and 7,500 B.C. are even larger than those of the Natufians. Nahal Oren, for example, is between 2,000 and 3,000 square meters, and that is one of the smallest. Gilgal, Tel Aswad, Netiv Hagdud, and the later Mureybit III are all larger than 8,000 square meters. Jericho, during that same time period, measures an astonishing 40,000 square meters and is estimated to have had well over 1,000 people dwelling there. As Bar-Yosef says: "The trend started with the Natufian . . . continued uninterruptedly through the 9th and 8th millennia B.C. It is one of the clearest cultural changes that took place in the prehistory of the Levant" (1982:30).

It is easy, however, to get a false impression of the overall picture. The groups that had chosen to, and succeeded in, living in one place all year round, whose population was increasing, did not represent the totality of the way of life of those millennia. Most of the population probably continued to live a seasonally mobile existence, moving from their winter to their summer camps. And let us remind ourselves again that all of them, sedentary and mobile groups alike, continued to depend on hunting animals and collecting wild plants for food. Food production is not in evidence whatsoever prior to 8,500 B.C. and debatably so in the following millennium.

The sedentary groups demand our attention, however, because that is the life style that prevailed more and more in all parts of the world. The consequences of the local population increase for these sedentary communities must have been considerable. A highly desirable site that made sedentary existence easy for a group of, say, 50 persons, may have been capable of sustaining 150 individuals given a gradual increase in the effectiveness of exploiting the local food resources and even greater reliance on storable foods as the population gradually grew. The same site, however, might no longer have been desirable, or even a possible site, for maintaining a group numbering 250 or 300 or more.

It would not have been easy, after a few centuries of sedentary living, for communities to split into two or more groups, not as easy as for mobile groups. If, in unusual circumstances, a seasonally mobile group became too large for convenient food collecting, it could rather easily split into, say, two familial groupings during one of their seasonal movements to a new camp which, in any event, had to be established or reestablished. In a sedentary group, if the issue arose, the question of who stayed and who left would have been momentous. It could have happened, of course. Some subgroups might have "budded off" and established themselves in some other favorable site. A return to a mobile existence seems even less likely. After perhaps twenty generations of sedentary existence was it even possible to return to mobile life? How many customs had changed? How many things had been forgotten? It seems more likely that efforts would have been made, one way or another, to sustain whatever population they had accumulated.

Some locations were able to sustain much larger populations than others. Jericho, for example, situated on a very fertile alluvial plain, between two large wadis that each year carried new soil and water into the plain, with a spring that provided a large perennial supply of water, and within easy reach of mountains and lowlands, was able to grow very large. On the other hand, the site of 'Eynan never grew past about 150 people and was abandoned by about 9,000 B.C.

Humans have the capacity, and apparently the inclination, to breed with little constraint. In this they are no different from any other animal, and it would be surprising if they did not show this characteristic. Prolific and successful reproduction is too closely linked to species survival for such a characteristic not to exist in any organism that has evolved successfully. A species that is lackadaisical about breeding might survive for a while under very benign conditions but even occasional adverse circumstances could easily lead to its extinction.

The population of any given species is, as everyone knows, held in check by competition with other species for food resources, by predators, and by available food supplies. If the population increases beyond the capacity of the ecological conditions, the death rate for that species will rise spectacularly. But this is not so for the human. The human is able, sooner or later, to find or invent solutions to problems. He is not restricted to any one climate or territory: he can live wherever he chooses. He has expanded his food supply by developing new foods and by cooking. He has invented tools and traps to enormously increase his effectiveness as a hunter. And there is no truly effective human predator, except other humans.

Human population, for a very long time, was held in check by internal biological mechanisms, undoubtedly aided somewhat by cultural practices that developed out of the necessity of maintaining mobility. Such was undoubtedly the case during the millions of years of human evolution and continued with the appearance of Modern man. It may or may not be relevant but Sussman (1972) points out that modern gorillas in the wild typically have live birth spacing of between four and five years, quite similar to human mobile populations.

The abandonment of a mobile pattern of existence in favor of sedentary life largely removed the internal biological checks on human reproduction. The human population began to increase sharply, presenting a problem which has been "solved" again and again but which is still with us.

Humans have great talents for solving problems that they themselves have unwittingly brought about. The early solution to the problems we have been discussing was food production and, like most of our solutions, brought further problems into being.

CHAPTER SEVEN
Toward Food Production

THE earliest dates at which human groups seriously attempted to produce food, rather than simply hunt and collect it, is not really determinable. First of all, some years would elapse between the start of such activities and the time that it would be recognizable in the remains that archaeologists dig up. Second, if it were carried out on a very small scale, the evidences of agricultural practices may not have survived. It is in this sense that it is debatable whether or not some settlements produced food during the period between 8,500 and 7,500 B.C. By 7,000 B.C., however, it is clear from numerous sites in western Asia that humans were deliberately producing food— planting, tending, and harvesting cereal grains; breeding, rearing, and slaughtering domesticated animals. By about 5,500 B.C. food that they themselves produced represented a major portion of what the occupants of settled communities ate.

If we dispassionately divorce ourselves from what, to us, is normal, obvious practice, and is, consequently, good, sensible, advantageous, and right, we can see that the whole activity of food production makes very little sense in terms of efficiency or convenience. It takes much more work to cultivate plants and animals than to collect and hunt the wild varieties. Harlan, in a much-quoted article, describes how he went out with a stone-bladed sickle, such as was used 9,000 years ago, to harvest wild wheat. In one hour he collected enough to yield a kilo of clean grain. He estimates that in a three-week period an experienced family "without even working very hard, could gather more grain than the family could possibly consume in a year" (1967:198). Furthermore, the wild wheat was much richer in protein than domesticated varieties.

And wild wheat was not the only food available, of course. Fruit (in season), nuts, wild vegetables, barley and many other edible plant foods could easily be collected in the appropriate season. Fishing and hunting also provided considerable food without a great deal of effort. Contemporary groups that still live on hunting and gathering do very well, even though they have been pushed into very marginal habitats.

Chagnon and Hames (1979) have calculated that the protein intake from hunting and fishing alone is quite adequate in such current groups. The humans who lived 9,000 years ago had hunting and fishing techniques that were probably quite as effective as these modern groups and, in addition, lived in locations where game was much more plentiful.

Food production was a momentous step which, once it had an appreciable foothold, could not be abandoned—it was irreversible. How did it start? Why did it start? Why did it continue? The early beginnings of the experiments, innovations, and practices that ultimately led to food production, go back in time a considerable way and, so, we will go back to the earliest times to see if we can answer any of our questions. The story is different for plants and for animals, although the motivations and objectives were similar, so we will take them one at a time.

First, animals. Providing food was not simply a problem of finding it, and in the case of an animal, killing it and bringing it back to the campsite. There was an interlocking problem of preserving it. If a hunting party killed and brought back, say, two gazelles, the meat available to the group did not consist of two gazelles: it consisted of how much gazelle meat could be eaten by the small group before the meat spoiled and was no longer edible. It is no accident that so much human effort and experiment has gone into trying to find ways to preserve food. Effective techniques of drying and smoking meat were inventions that may have already made their appearance in the period with which we begin, between 20,000 and 15,000 years ago.

There was, however, one way to preserve meat perfectly that must have been discovered very early by ingenious humans—don't kill the animal. Capturing two gazelles is much better than killing two gazelles. You can keep them tethered or penned until you are ready to kill them, one at a time. And it costs you almost nothing to keep a few of them alive until you are ready to eat them. Gazelles, deer, goats, sheep, and cattle do not compete with humans for food. They are able to, and do, eat cellulose, which humans are unable to digest. These animals, whose meat humans can digest, have internal mechanisms for fermenting the cellulose and digesting the fermentation products. So the captured, tethered animal can be kept alive by simply allowing it to graze, in the near vicinity, on plants that the human does not care about.

It is clear to those who have looked for evidence that this was indeed done. Sturdy, after extensive analysis of the data from numerous German sites dating back to the last glacial period, summarizes the reindeer hunting practices by concluding "that the animals required for one season are separated and kept near at hand, and that the movements of the main herd from which those animals are drawn are kept under observation" (1975:93).

Bahn (1978, 1980) argues that capturing and keeping animals alive for a time was a prevalent practice in western Europe, perhaps even dating back to late Homo sapiens. He claims that many engravings of horse heads and of reindeer indicate the use of "harness" to restrain, and perhaps control, the animal. He also points out that some animal skulls have been found which were killed "with such precision that the animal must have been under control at the time" (1978:189). Perhaps the most compelling evidence comes from finds of teeth of horses that are worn down in a way that never occurs with horses that run free: "Only horses which are subjected to 'prolonged restraint,' i.e., which are tied up or stabled, wear down their teeth in this particular way" (p. 189). Similar practices of capturing and preserving animals for food must have been widespread before there was any "domestication" of the animals.

The move from this elegant means of preserving meat to the most rudimentary forms of animal husbandry was a very small step and must have seemed effortless. Occasionally, a birth would have occurred among the animals rounded up and awaiting slaughter. Thus, one could easily increase the number of animals available for food by postponing the slaughter of females. Hunting and capturing new animals continued, of course. The hunters had simply found a way to increase the yield with relatively little additional work.

It is not difficult to imagine that human groups would have taken advantage, increasingly, of this rather effortless means of storing their supply of meat. Soon, here and there, the practice would have shaded into what we think of as animal husbandry, maintaining the mature female animals, not for eventual slaughter for food, but for the purposes of producing new animals that would be eaten. This gradual, perhaps almost imperceptible, change required the realization, however, that some animals reproduce better in captivity than others, a realization that would not have been difficult to achieve.

Animals that reproduced well in captivity would, naturally, have gradually come to be preferred even though the communities continued to rely primarily on those animals that were most plentiful and easiest to hunt and capture. My guess is that the gazelle, very prevalent in western Asia, does not reproduce well in captivity. It is instructive that throughout the Levant, from the earliest Kebaran sites (about 17,000 B.C.) through the Natufian period and well into pre-pottery Neolithic A times (about 7,000 B.C.), the major source of meat was, almost uniformly, the gazelle. With the first clear evidence of animal domestication, however, the major meat source had changed to sheep and goats, both wild and domesticated (Bar-Yosef 1982: fig 11).

Second, plants. The roots of plant domestication also go far back in time, as far back as the earliest use of cereal grain for food. And there is evidence from which we can infer that ground cereal grains were in use longer ago than 15,000 B.C. The major evidence consists of stones used for grinding and stone tools possessing a sheen characteristically caused by cutting grasses (Bar-Yosef 1980), but the inference is further strengthened by the occasional finds of cereal grains that date that far back, for example, in the Kebaran level of Nahal Oren (Van Zeist 1976) and in Wadi Kubbaniya (Wendorf and Schild 1980).

At the beginning of its use, cereal grains represented only a tiny fraction of the food supply in some places and many sites show no evidence at all of cereal grain consumption. One can wonder why humans ever started to use wheat and barley as food. One not only has to gather the seeds but one then has to separate them from the husks, dry them and, in addition, grind them. Diversification of the food supply as a deliberate intention is, of course, a possible reason. It conceivably may also have simply reflected the human predilection for a variety of tastes. Anyone who has watched some person eating unshelled sunflower seeds, for example, has to wonder, in the same way, why they do it—it is clearly not for the value of the food intake.

Whatever the reason, it is clear that human groups were playing around with cereal grains for at least five or six thousand years before they began to rely appreciably on them in the Natufian era of the Levant. It is not unimaginable that during this long period of time, humans discovered, probably again and again, that one could, if one wanted to, deliberately plant the seeds and thereby control where the wheat and barley grew. Humans, with their uncontrollable urges to experiment and explore and manage events, must have tried many ways to grow various kinds of plant food.

Indeed, Wendorf and Schild (1980) believe they have uncovered evidence of deliberate cultivation dating back to 16,000 B.C. They found carbonized grains of wheat and barley in a campsite in a wadi of the Nile valley where, they believe, wild barley would not have grown naturally. In addition, microscopic examination reveals a similarity of these grains to those of domesticated varieties. The evidence that these carbonized grains are domesticated rather than wild varieties is not totally compelling but is reasonable. The solidity of the evidence, and the extent to which one can still doubt if one wants to, is well illustrated by Wendorf and Schild:

> One of the Wadi Kubbaniya grains (einkorn wheat) was still attached to the rachilla. Stemler and Falk used a scanning electron microscope to compare this grain with examples of wild and domestic wheat. These photographs indicate that the base on the Kubbaniya examples does not have a smooth abscission zone, but has a protruding rough fracture surface as in the domestic variety. *Unfortunately, however, the abscission zone in wild wheat is not complete until the grain is mature, so that wild wheat harvested green and domesticated wheat would have the same rough fracture as the Kubbaniya specimen.* (1980:276; italics added)

All in all, the authors conclude that, considering the congruence of many factors, these grains do represent domesticated varieties, the results of man himself, planting and harvesting the grain. If they are correct, and their arguments are strong, then even 18,000 years ago some group went through a period of a minor amount of food production. How many times this kind of thing occurred is impossible to say—my guess would be many. The conditions for preservation of fossil grain are not very good in the area in which it was most likely to have happened and, until recently, excavators have not looked for such evidence with determination. Let us accept as fact, knowing some of the characteristics of humans, that for as long as they were using cereal grains they were also, here and there, experimenting with deliberate production.

The interesting point is that over this long period of about ten thousand years of use of such cereal grains and, probably, occasional experiments with deliberately growing them, the practice of food production did not take hold. Even when, with the onset of sedentary groups, the reliance on cereal grains increased markedly, they still gathered the wild varieties—they did not plant, tend and produce their own. Actually, there was little to be gained by plant food production, and it involved more work. The only advantages to be obtained would be to reduce the time taken to locate the wild food and to have denser stands of wheat or barley closer to the camp. By planting, more of the cereal grain would grow on a given piece of land than would normally occur without human intervention. But the wild stands of cereal grasses were dense enough, and the efforts needed for food production, clearing land, planting and tending, were considerable. In addition, if they were to produce the food rather than simply harvest wild crops they would have had to plant and harvest much more than they needed for food. A large proportion of the harvest of grain would have to be safely stored away in order to be able to plant the next year's crop.

From this point of view it is not at all surprising that for about ten thousand years, humans used cereal grains but did not seriously pursue plant food production in a sustained manner. But we know that finally they did. Excavations dating to the seventh millennium before the Christian era reveal numerous indications of plant and animal food production in western Asia on at least a small scale. The main sources of food continued to be wild animals and wild plants, however, and deliberate production probably accounted for no more than 5 or 10 percent of the food supply in most cases. By the sixth millennium, though, food production had increased in importance and gradually it became the main source of food.

How and why did this happen? For what reasons did humans, who had rejected it for so long, finally venture into and persist in producing their own food? As you might imagine, this is not a new question. Many answers have been provided. There was a time when food production was seen as a great revolutionary event that for the first time provided humans with a reliable, stable, and ample food supply, thus permitting humans to settle down and allowing the development of great societies. As recently as 1960 Braidwood and Howe, for example, said: "The appearance of the village-farming community marked a transition, in cultural history, of great import for what was to follow. Before it were some half a million years of savagery during which small wandering bands of people . . . led an essentially 'natural' catch-as-catch-can existence" (p. 1).

We now know that humans were settling down long before they produced their own food, that their food supply was quite adequate, and that food production was far from being either a sudden event or an unalloyed blessing. No one today would still express such views. Explanation has, hence, changed its character. Some, emphasizing the gradual nature of the growth of food production, see no need to explain much. Hawkes, for example says: "there was no incentive involved in the three stages of agriculture as I have set them out, . . . the process, once started was practically automatic . . . gathering changed imperceptibly into harvesting and thence into planting" (1969:27). As gradual as it may have been, however, one still wants to understand how and why it happened.

Recently, there has been an increased tendency to explain the transition to food production on the basis of ecological pressures. The clearest, most extreme position is the one taken by Cohen (1977), who argues that food production developed in response to a serious food shortage due to rapidly increasing population. And he bolsters his argument by interpreting the diversification of the food supply, prior to agriculture, as indicating a food shortage that forced humans to eat foods that they would not have eaten in circumstances of plenty. Others, such as Binford, (1968) and Flannery (1969) offer essentially the same explanation in much less extreme form. They argue that food production would not have been taken up in locations that were desirable but would have been started first by groups living in marginal locations—again motivated by a food shortage, although only a local food shortage in this version.

These explanations focusing on crises of food supply probably have elements of truth to them, but they point up what amounts to a paradox concerning the origins of agriculture. Food production, plant and animal, could not conceivably have begun in the midst of a serious scarcity of food—it could only have started in the midst of a plentiful food supply. In the Levant this is very clear. Sedentary populations were established and farming began in areas with a Mediterranean climate while the populations of the more marginal, desertic regions continued to hunt and gather.

In the absence of plenty one does not experiment with vital food supplies. Food production requires a surplus of considerable magnitude. The animals that are left alive to breed next year and the seed that is stored away to be planted next year are all foods that cannot be eaten. Imagine a group of humans, faced with a serious food shortage, who would continue to endure serious hunger without eating whatever food was available. Humans do not do this—except, perhaps, if prevented from eating by force. Indeed, this consumption of any available food when there is hunger is one of the reasons that famine in an area is usually an enduring affair lasting many years if help from the outside does not come. The people in the area in which there is a food shortage eat up their reserve of seeds and their breeding animals, making recovery in subsequent years difficult.

The thousands of years of dabbling and experimenting with plant and animal food production would, indeed, have occurred only during times of plenty. Human curiosity would have impelled it, and the lure of controling the food supply would have been powerful, at least that is my conception of the nature of the human animal. Considering everything, however, it is not surprising that for thousands of years human groups, with an already plentiful food supply, did not find it worthwhile to persist for very long in a dubious agricultural enterprise.

In the past few pages we seem to have come up with some reasonable understanding of why human groups did *not* engage in agriculture but preferred to rely on wild plants and animals. In short, we have not yet come to grips with the paradox; we have yet to explain why, eventually, humans did begin to produce their own food on a consistent basis. For this to have happened, the supply of wild food had to continue to be plentiful. And if it was plentiful, why the extra work and labor of producing it? To try to grapple with this problem, let us first review the specific benefits, few that they may be, of producing plant and animal food. Wild animals roam free and are not as densely packed together as can be achieved with captive animals, even with the captive animals depending for their own food entirely on wild, naturally growing plants. This would be true, of course, as long as the number of captive animals used for food production does not grow too large. So animal husbandry, on a small scale, could enlarge the food supply concentrated in a small locality.

Plant food production provided precisely the same benefit. With planting and tending, denser stands of wheat and barley could be produced than occurred naturally with the wild varieties. Again, the food supply concentrated in a small area could be increased; that is about all—higher yields per unit of land. But we are talking about a time when the human population in western Asia was still not large and land was not scarce. Later on, other advantages of food production appeared but they were primarily fortuitous: they took time to appear and they could not have influenced the beginnings of agriculture.

For example, sheep were certainly not initially husbanded for their wool. Wild sheep do not have much wool: their coats are hairy rather than woolly. After many, many generations of breeding in captivity domestic sheep develop woolly coats for reasons no one seems to understand. As another example, domesticated wheat eventually tends to have larger seeds than wild wheat (although less rich in protein), thus increasing even more the food yield per unit of land. And six-rowed barley, which eventually appears under conditions of domestication, obviously provides more food than wild two-rowed barley. But these changes took centuries and centuries to appear.

Such future unanticipated benefits aside, we are left still with only the advantage of greater concentration of food per unit of land. But this advantage may, indeed, have been pivotal. Food production in this part of the world began only after some human groups had settled down to year-round residence in one place and the local populations of those settlements had grown to sizes previously unheard of. If we want to imagine that this unanticipated local population increase would have strained the food resources of the area, even in exceptionally desirable locations, we must keep in mind what kind of area we are imagining about. The increase in population would primarily have necessitated hunting and gathering over somewhat larger distances, perhaps inconveniently large but not impossibly so. However, under these circumstances, though hunting and gathering over a rather extended area were still capable of supplying an abundant amount of food, techniques of increasing the food yield per unit of land, in an area near the settlement, may have seemed attractive.

The extra burdens would, at the beginning, not have proved very onerous. These people did not change their way of life. They were still hunters and gatherers and storers of food: no other characterization is possible. Food production provided, probably, less than 5 percent of the food. In short, very little food was deliberately produced, perhaps just enough to shrink to more convenient size the area within which food was hunted and gathered. The work involved in such a small amount of agriculture would have seemed very small for the community as a whole, and the overproduction needed for continued agriculture would not have been of aggravating proportions. In bad years they simply again extended the area in which they hunted and gathered.

Agriculture did not burst upon the scene as a marvelous solution to an urgent problem. The earliest clear evidence of domesticated plants and animals, about 7,000 B.C., does not, of course, represent the beginning of agriculture. It would have taken some considerable time for the domesticated varieties to develop the singular morphological characteristics that mark them clearly as domestic and not wild. There was no rush toward agriculture. The difficulties and problems must have gradually become more and more apparent. It took at least two thousand years after the first known beginnings before food production was widespread, providing as much as 40 percent to 50 percent of the food supply in the settled communities. And we should also remember that even then, say, 5,000 B.C., not all humans lived in settled communities. We cannot know the proportion but, certainly, many still lived in small groups, seasonally mobile, getting all of their food by hunting and gathering.

We still have not, however, disposed of the problem; we have not resolved the paradox. To say that something developed gradually over two to three thousand years explains nothing—it simply says it took a long time. Why did it continue to spread? Why did it gradually become the major source of food for human groups? Consider the problems that agriculture created, solutions to which have resulted in practices that are almost absurd. As reliance on domesticated animals for meat increased, the size of herds had to increase, of necessity. A large number of animals cannot, of course, graze incessantly in the near vicinity of the village. Either the animals had to be moved, at least seasonally, from place to place, or the humans had to bring food to the animals. Ultimately, they even had to work to produce the food that they brought to the animals to eat. Meat thus eventually became the most expensive kind of food for humans. As one person remarked to me once, unfortunately I have forgotten who, the majority of humans living today are involuntary vegetarians.

Increased reliance on domesticated cereal grains also created problems. Land on which wild varieties thrived, mainly hilly areas, was not necessarily the kind of land on which food production could be most conveniently practiced. Land suitable for agriculture started to become a rare resource. When humans resorted to artificial irrigation to increase the yield and the reliability of the crops, suitable land became even scarcer. The amount of work involved in food production increased considerably, and the need for an organized work force emerged.

Perhaps, all this happened so gradually, so imperceptibly, that no one noticed. It seems far more likely that two factors combined to make the progression inevitable. Continued local population increase would have pushed for more and more reliance on the greater yields per unit of land that agriculture could provide. But even more important, as we will see in the next chapter, was the fact that agriculture, once started on even a relatively small scale, was irreversible, in principle, because of the ecological changes it wrought. Even if populations suffered drastic declines, and this certainly must have happened locally from time to time, people could no longer easily revert to hunting wild animals and gathering wild plant food.

The consequences of food production, certainly unforeseen and, largely, unforeseeable, were to produce enduring changes in the way humans lived and how they organized their communities.

CHAPTER EIGHT
The Consequences of Food Production

M OST people today think of agriculture, both plant and animal, as having produced a revolution (which it did) of great benefit to mankind (which is at least debatable). Actually, it could not have been a simple, uncomplicated, beneficial process as the practice of agriculture continued and grew. At the same time that the increasing practice of food production solved, or minimized, the impact of some problems, it created new problems that were serious. While some of these new problems took hundreds or even thousands of years to develop, others would have shown up in the space of only a few years. A brief look at some of these new problems will raise for us the question as to why the practice, as perilous and effortful as it became, was not abandoned but, on the contrary, continued to expand.

The early serious attempts at prolonged planting and harvesting of cereal grains must have been disastrous. As long as humans relied on collecting wild plants, they would not have known that soil wears out. Once they started planting seeds year after year in the same place, however, trouble would have appeared. By the third or fourth year of replanting the harvested crop would probably have been meager, unless the land lay in an alluvial area, the soil replenished by floods each year. Then it would have taken longer for the soil to wear out. It is not possible to know how long it took for humans to discover that land has to lie fallow periodically. Until they discovered this, harvests would have been very unsatisfactory and after they discovered it they would need much more suitable land than they had previously imagined. Flannery points out that "Today in Khuzistan, three-fourths of all arable land is fallow during any given year" (1969:88).

These difficulties would have been compounded by the great variability of rainfall from year to year. Flannery (1969) estimates the average yield of wheat today in Khuzistan to be 410 kilos per hectare. This average, however, is made up of yields that, in a very good year, could be as high as 1,000 kilos per hectare and in bad years could be almost nothing. These hazardous conditions for dry farming apply all over the Near East: agriculture did not, in most places, offer a means of obtaining a reliable food supply. There were also other sources of occasional disaster. Watson (1966), for example, states that the farmers she talked to in Iranian Kurdistan reported that their entire wheat crop in 1958, 1959, and 1960 had been destroyed by insects. Early groups of people who tried farming must have given up many times but, obviously, they tried again and again.

We must repeat that these human groups, with their ingenuity and their penchant for controlling their environment, experimented and tried and tried again in a situation where food was plentiful and at a time in which the products, both plant and animal, of such food production amounted to between 5 and 10 percent of the food consumed. They were experimenting under conditions in which the frequent agricultural catastrophes were not, to them, disasters. Worn-out soil, inadequate rainfall, and the like did not unduly affect their food supply. Like humans do, they tried various things, learned what to do and what not to do. If only 5 to 10 percent of the food supply was involved, a disastrous agricultural year or two could be coped with in an area of abundance—other foods could be used; hunting and gathering over a wider area could be pursued.

The preceding discussion of the hazards of food production has a specious ring to it, however. Apart from the problem of the soil becoming less fertile, necessitating the fallowing of land, would not the perils of inadequate rainfall, insect invasions or whatever other scourge one wants to dream up, have affected wild plants as well as domesticated ones? There obviously must be another part to the argument, namely, the assertion or assumption that the wild food supply was more stable and less hazardous than a domesticated food supply. The validity of this assumption must be examined, of course.

The first point that must be made is that if a plant, such as wheat or barley, flourishes in a wild state in a given area, this is proof that the particular plant is well adapted to that area and can, and does, survive whatever climatic fluctuations or pestilences occur. In some years, of course, the wild stands might be denser and more extensive than in other years; in some years the wild plant might flourish best 100 meters farther uphill or downhill—but the wild plant does survive. Year after year there will be available some quantity of food from this plant.

The next question, then, is how and in what ways does deliberate food production cause the plant to be more vulnerable to environmental fluctuations. There are two ways in which agriculture contributed to making cultivated plants less hardy. One of these is quite simple. The areas in which the wild plant flourishes best are frequently not the most convenient areas for deliberate planting. Wild wheat and barley, for example, grew abundantly in very hilly areas at altitudes in which the temperature and rainfall particularly suited them, but such hilly terrains would have made planting and tending more arduous. If the human attempts to cultivate the plant in an area away from where it grows wild, the plant will, initially at least, be less well adapted to the new area. While it might grow reasonably well in a year that was very benign for the plant, other years might be ruinous. The very fact that the wild plant had not spontaneously spread to a given area means that the plant was not, in its wild state, well adapted to the conditions there. If the plant survived at all in this new area, it would have been by means of a process of natural and human selection that gradually altered the plant. In difficult years those individual plants that did mature and produce seed would have been ones that had genetic characteristics that enabled them to survive. They would have survived, however, in an environment compounded with human intervention—the plant would still, most likely, be more vulnerable to environmental changes.

The other contribution of agriculture to the vulnerability of plants is somewhat more complicated. Human intervention in the process means that genetic changes will occur in any plant even if the deliberate cultivation occurs within the area in which the wild plant naturally flourishes. For a wild plant to be successful there must be some mechanism for widespread scattering of its seed. In the case of wheat and barley this mechanism is simple. The head that contains the seeds is very brittle and as soon as those seeds are ripe the head fractures and the small light seeds scatter. As long as humans collected these wild cereal grains, this characteristic was maintained, probably even enhanced. Those individual plants whose seed heads were somewhat tougher and held together longer after ripening were more likely to get collected by the human, thus removing them from the population of seeds that replanted themselves.

With deliberate cultivation, however, this process reversed itself automatically. The seeds that the cultivator planted were, obviously, the seeds that he harvested, namely, those with a tougher seed head and, probably, those with larger seeds. And so, domesticated wheat and barley became morphologically and genetically different from their wild ancestors. This much is clear and factually supported. Domesticated varieties of these cereal grains had larger seeds which did not scatter when ripe or when harvested. But why would these domesticated varieties be less hardy than the wild plants? Because the wild plant, inevitably, selects itself for reproduction simply by virtue of its survivability in the natural environment, whatever the vicissitudes. The selection processes that changed these wild plants into domesticated ones had only partly to do with survivability: principally it was governed by a human agency—which seeds he was most likely to collect and then plant and tend. That selection factor does not guarantee hardiness.

We have still not answered the question of why the deliberate cultivation of cereal grains not only persisted but grew in importance, providing an increasingly large proportion of the plant food consumed by humans. Crop failures that were not disastrous to a community that depended on wild animals and wild plants for 90 to 95 percent of its food would, however, very seriously affect a community that relied much more heavily, say, 40 to 50 percent, on cultivated crops. Of course, by the time human groups arrived at such heavy dependence on agriculture, they had learned more about how to do it successfully, but catastrophes undoubtedly continued to occur. Part of the answer to the question of why agriculture grew to such dangerous proportions certainly lies in the continued increase in the population of the sedentary communities. It became increasingly necessary to have higher yields per unit of land within reasonable access of the settlement, and this advantage agriculture could provide when successful although at the cost of considerable work and risk.

This was not, however, the only factor or even the major factor. In addition, agriculture grew more and more because the human intervention in the process of growth and reproduction made agriculture, once started, intrinsically irreversible. Humans, in the course of cultivating plants and trying to find ways to improve and control more effectively the food supply from these plants, effectively changed the natural distribution of wild plants in the areas in which they lived.

Domesticated plants and wild plants do not coexist easily. Left on their own, without human intervention, the wild plants would quickly overrun and replace the domesticated varieties. This implies, however, that for the human cultivator, the wild variety of the plant he had domesticated became a weed. For the domesticated plant to prosper, the wild variety had to be eradicated in the vicinity of the settlement. In the course of several hundred years human groups would no longer have had a choice of producing or gathering wheat and barley. If one wanted those cereal grains, and they must have been highly desirable because of the ease of storage, one had to cultivate them—the wild varieties were largely gone.

The effects of the cultivation of wheat and barley were not restricted to the wild varieties of only those two grains. Any wild plants, as Flannery points out, "that have the same general growing season as wheat and barley . . . and also compete for the same alluvial soil with low salinity which the cereals require . . . assumed the status of weeds and were removed to make way for cultivated grains" (1969:88). The total effect was not only to make grain production necessary, but also to reduce the variety of plant foods available to these people.

We should remind ourselves that what was happening in the long run was probably not very obvious in the short run. We are not dealing with sudden changes or with brief periods of time. From the earliest beginnings of sustained plant cultivation to the time when cultivated wheat and barley were a very appreciable part of the food supply took more than two thousand years in western Asia. And during this whole period food from wild plants grew scarcer and scarcer. Humans did not turn away from wild food sources voluntarily. Indeed, they continued to rely on them to the extent that they were available. Flannery (1969) points out an interesting example. In Iran there was a plant with an edible pod that did not compete with the cereal grains. The plant, Prosopis, matures in a different season of the year and has a deep root system so that it can even survive plowing. The consumption of this wild plant, contrary to others, did increase during the period from about 7,000 to 5,500 b.c.

To summarize, let us, once more, ask the question: what advantages did food production offer over food gathering? It did not ensure a more stable food supply in the long run. On the contrary, the food supply was more variable from good year to bad year and the variety of food was reduced. It did not make it easier to obtain food. Plowing or hoeing, planting, weeding and harvesting involved much more work than locating the best stands of wild grains and harvesting those. It did not make for an improvement in the diet: the wild varieties were as rich, or richer, in protein than the domesticated plants. As Flannery summarizes: "The only real advantage of cereal cultivation is that it increases carrying capacity of the land in terms of kilograms per hectare" (1969:86). Thus, communities could, and did, increase in size. More food could be produced close to one site, but this was not the major incentive for cereal grain cultivation—rather it was one of the results. The difficulties increased considerably: the necessity of fallowing land and the uncertainty of rainfall in proper amounts, properly timed, made dry farming very risky. These risks were, of course, aggravated as cereal grains became a more important food source, as the availability of wild plant food diminished, and as villages grew in size. There came a time when dry farming could no longer do the job: crop failures were catastrophic.

Humans have always been ingenious in solving such problems although the solutions frequently created other unanticipated problems. The solution that was invented to eliminate the hazards of dry farming was irrigation. Extensive irrigation, however, was not possible everywhere. It required alluvial plains associated with rivers. The Nile valley in Egypt, with the natural irrigation provided by annual flooding, was ideal for this purpose. In western Asia the lowlands through which streams carried the runoff from the Zagros mountains were also suitable, especially the valleys in southern Mesopotamia along the Tigris and Euphrates rivers. Such areas, easily irrigated, were naturally the places where the first "civilizations" emerged: along the Nile, in the Tigris-Euphrates valleys, in the Indus valley in India, and in the great central river valleys of China.

In places where irrigation was not feasible there were great difficulties as a result of the dependence on agriculture for food. The levantine regions that saw the beginnings of this process provide a good case in point. According to Bar-Yosef, during a discussion, evidence increasingly suggests that there was a drying, a diminution in rainfall, in the southern Levant that started sometime during the late seventh millennium B.C. This would have wrecked the dry farming enterprise there and it is true that the development of village-farming communities virtually ceased in that area during that time. Major development of such settlements that depended on dry farming continued in the much rainier northern regions of Anatolia. For the people who had inhabited the growing sedentary villages of the Levant, this period must have produced considerable prolonged hardship.

Irrigation did offer a solution to the problem of cultivating cereal grain. Canals to carry water from the rivers to the cultivated fields offered a much more reliable method of watering crops than depending on rainfall. In the river plains of Mesopotamia this solution was so successful that, in time, huge areas were irrigated in this manner, canals to transport water from the rivers to the land extending farther and farther from the water source and eventually criss-crossing the land.

The success, and the ultimate failure, of the irrigation solution are both vividly illustrated in southern Mesopotamia. With irrigation the land produced even more kilograms of food per hectare than with dry farming and population centers could, and did, increase more in size. An organized and coordinated work force became even more important: canals had to be dug, maintained, and freed from silting; grain had to be planted over a wide area at the appropriate time of the year; and all of the harvesting had to be done in a brief three-week period. It is no accident that southern Mesopotamia saw the emergence of one of the earliest highly structured societies, namely, Sumer.

Perhaps it is a distortion to talk of the failure of irrigation. A solution that is effective, more or less, for over two thousand years is quite an achievement. But problems there were. Wild plant food became even scarcer—wheat and barley became the dominant, staple food. But two things happened to the land. As Helbaek puts it: "With the immense increase of surface subjected to silt deposition and a corresponding surface of water in canals and fields exposed to evaporation, the chemical composition of the arable land was fundamentally changed and the gradually raised level of the land reduced the amount of water available for irrigation" (1969:194).

The silting and consequent elevation of the cultivated land relative to the height of the rivers made it more and more difficult to bring the water to the land. But of even greater consequence was the increased salinity of the soil caused by silting and evaporation. Gradually, the land became too saline to sustain some crops. Wheat is less tolerant of saline soil and over the course of two thousand years wheat almost disappeared as a crop in Mesopotamia. It grew only where new lands were brought into irrigated agriculture. Barley was the major crop for a long time, but it too will not grow if the soil becomes too filled with salts. "In the long run barley also failed, and the whole land was practically deserted" (Helbaek 1969:195).

So far I have concentrated this discussion on the cultivation of the cereal grains, but animal husbandry was also an integral part of food production and needs to be examined. As said earlier, animal husbandry probably developed easily and almost effortlessly from animal capture and confinement as a means of food storage. Indeed, the major problem in domesticating animals to produce meat for food may have been simply to locate those species that were tractable and reproduced well in captivity. I have already referred to the fact that gazelle bones, by far, outnumber any other species in excavations in the southern Levant from Kebaran cultures (13,000 B.C.) through the time of the "pre-pottery Neolithic A" designation (7,500 B.C.). Yet, the gazelle was never domesticated. Starting about 7,000 B.C. there is a sharp diminution of gazelle bones. Instead, the bones of sheep and goats, showing signs of domestication, predominate. And this is not, of course, the only example one can point to. Clutton-Brock (1969) and Kurten (1965) both found large numbers of remains of foxes in very early (Pre-Neolithic) sites in the Levant. Yet the fox does not emerge as a domesticated animal. Similarly, in Europe, reindeer were herded but not domesticated (Sturdy 1975).

Such differences among animals in the manner in which they adapt to captivity are intriguing. In the course of the last twelve thousand years or so, man has undoubtedly attempted to domesticate a huge variety of animals, either for food production or for work purposes. Only a small number have succumbed, however—goats, sheep, cattle, pigs, dogs, horses, camels, water-buffalo, mink, chickens, pigeons, and a few others. In other instances, man has not succeeded. Hawks can be trained to perform certain things but they cannot be reared in captivity. Similarly, gibbons have been captured and trained to climb trees to harvest coconuts but when one dies another must be captured from the wild: they too do not successfully reproduce when confined. Fascinating as this issue is, it is a small digression from the present concern, so I will return to the major issue.

As happened with plants those animals that were domesticated became different, morphologically, from their wild ancestors. In plants, however, there was an easily understandable relationship between the morphological changes that occurred and the conditions and requirements of the process of domestication. In animals this relation is rather obscure. It is true that domestic varieties tended to be smaller than the wild varieties, and this might reflect the greater ease with which humans might have been able to control smaller animals. But, in the main, the nature of the changes is bewildering.

Domesticated goats have twisted horns, a form not found in the wild. Wild sheep are predominantly hairy; heavy wool coats only develop in domesticated sheep. In domesticated pigs the shape of the skull is different from the wild variety. None of these, or of numerous other examples, seems clearly related to a process of domestication.

Obviously, there was selection, and strong selection, of which animals were bred and which were not, which were kept alive and which were killed—but the changes we know about seem like incidental accompaniments of whatever factors were operating.

But again, as in the case of plants, because of the intervention of man, the domestic and wild varieties did not coexist well together. Humans hunted and killed the wild while preserving and breeding the domesticated variety. Since the wild and the domesticated animals preferred the same terrain and sought the same food, the existence of the wild progenitor in the vicinity of the domesticated animal was undesirable. Of necessity, as the process of domestication proceeded, hunting became less and less important in an irreversible way; after a time the wild varieties were no longer there to be hunted.

Animal husbandry, however, would not have produced the same severe problems as the cultivation of cereal grains; indeed it may not have presented many problems at all. Animal husbandry undoubtedly began in an aura of benign ease. As already stated, the two major early domesticates, goats and sheep, do not compete with humans for food (and the same is true for cattle). These animals can, and do, eat leaves and grasses that are high in cellulose and low in protein—a diet on which humans cannot live. As Reed points out, these animals have "internal fermentation vats" in which bacteria "process the ingested food and break down the cellulose to simpler molecules which are then available to the mammal's digestive system" (1969:365).

Of course, these domesticated animals had to be kept away from the cultivated fields of grain before the harvest, but this applied to the wild animals also. And this could not have been much of a problem—at least at the beginning there was plenty of land not suited for planting, on which the goats and sheep could graze. Even in years that yielded very poor grain harvests, the animals would have been relatively unaffected. After all, they were able to feed on wild plant cover, whatever happened to succeed in growing.

It is, perhaps, not too wild a speculation to imagine that the kind of nomadic existence still practiced by Bedouins and some others in parts of the world was a later adaptation, arising from the difficulties and failures of plant cultivation and the relative ease of animal husbandry. They abandoned plant agriculture and, keeping their animals, moved from one easy grazing area to another in very small groups.

The ease and simplicity of animal husbandry did not survive past the early stages of the growth of villages. As the population increased and the settlement grew larger, the size of the herd of domesticated animals needed to feed the people also grew. While it may have been a trivial matter to have ten or twenty goats and sheep grazing to their fill in the near vicinity of the village, this would have been a difficult problem for, say, one hundred animals. There would not have been enough natural forage within easy distance of a large village to support such a herd year after year. The larger supply of manpower for tending and herding the animals over longer distances to find forage made it possible for flocks to grow in size but animal husbandry became much more difficult and inconvenient.

There were, of course, many possible solutions to these problems of feeding large numbers of domesticated animals and, to be sure, they have all been tried. Outside of restricting the number of animals and having less meat to eat, a solution that has freqently been forced on people but never chosen voluntarily, all the solutions involved either bringing the animals to food or bringing food to the animals. Transhumance, the practice of bringing the animals to distant places uninhabited by humans for several months of the year at a time, still survives in many parts of the world. Otherwise, human groups had to collect food, and even grow food, to bring to the animals. While wild animals found their own food, man had to work to provide food for the domesticates.

The fact is that, with increasing population, none of these solutions worked well in western Asia and, in time, overgrazing contributed its share to producing disastrous effects on the land. This, together with cutting down trees for wood and the effects of intensive plant cultivation jointly operated to remove the natural plant cover, exposing the land to rapid erosion of the soil. Many parts of western Asia that had once been fertile eventually became man-made barren deserts.

Animal husbandry itself probably did not ever rival plant cultivation in the severity of the problems that were created. For one thing, there were useful by-products not available from wild animals. After a while, it is uncertain when, the wool that developed on domestic sheep became economically important and, of course, milk obtained from domestic sheep and goats provided an additional food supply. Cows milk did not make an impact until much later: cattle, domesticated from the wild aurochs, are not found at all until about 5,000 B.C. and were not widespread, as were goats and sheep, at that time.

Domesticated animals also were used to help solve the increasingly complex requirements for work and for transportation of food and other supplies. Cattle, according to Reed (1969), were the first domesticates that were able to do heavy labor such as pulling a plow and by about 3,500 B.C. one knows from pictorial representations that plows were in use in Mesopotamia. Other animals were also eventually domesticated and put to work to deal with the increasingly heavy demands. By about 3,000 B.C. the Syrian onager (a half-ass) was in use. Others such as the water buffalo and the camel appeared later. The horse does not appear as a domesticated animal in western Asia until about 2,000 B.C. (Drower 1969).

Domesticated animals thus represent the first successful harnessing of power to do some of the work demanded by the growth of populations in towns and the people's reliance on food production. These demands and the answers to the problems, however, introduced increasing complexities into the economic life, and also into the social structure, of human communities. The variety of tasks increased greatly and the need for organization was not far behind.

CHAPTER NINE
Technology, Trade, and Social Organization

F ROM the earliest times, the evidence is that human beings lived in groups. The functioning of these groups, the nature of the relations among members of a group, the distribution among them of the work of getting food are matters that are, however, not at all clear. Fossil bones, unfortunately, do not provide clues about social organization. One can only speculate, make inferences from seemingly rational arguments, or extrapolate backward from what we know about contemporary human groups, and, of course, writers have done all of these things.

It has been proposed, for example, that there has always been a division of labor between males and females. On the basis of a reasonably uniform pattern that exists in contemporary groups that still live by hunting and gathering wild foods, it is suggested that in human groups males always did the hunting of animals while women gathered plant food (Lee and DeVore 1968). Perhaps this was the case—arguments can be made for it. Certainly, only the woman could feed the infant at her breast and so would frequently have been somewhat more limited in her mobility. In addition, sexual dimorphism has existed in all human species: the males were larger than the females and, presumably, also stronger and swifter. All these factors may have made it easier and surer for the males to do the hunting.

But such arguments are weak. It is difficult to imagine that the small incremental strength and swiftness that the male possessed was an important factor in hunting. Surely, the male hunter did not outrun animals that were twice as swift as he. And if the woman did go hunting, she might have left the infant in the temporary care, for a few hours, of someone else in the group. It is possible, however, that such a division of labor between males and females did always exist. We do not and will not know. If it did always exist, then one might be tempted to speculate that it is because of a genetically relevant difference rather than a purely cultural difference that men enjoy hunting as a sport more than do women.

Other speculations about social organization in the very distant past are even less substantiated. Lovejoy (1981), for example, on the basis of some limiting assumptions, comes to the astonishing conclusion that the earliest humans were monogamous. It seems almost inconceivable to me that, considering the likely size of the human group (say between five and fifteen) and the conditions of existence two or three million years ago, that monogamy could have been a viable practice. Consider a group of ten humans, for example, four or five of them adult, who came into contact with other groups quite infrequently, perhaps only once or twice a year. It would not have been a rare occurrence, because of accidents of birth and accidents of mortality, for only one of the adults to be male, say. Monogamy under such circumstances?

In spite of the tenuous nature of speculation about prehistoric forms of social organization, the issues are important enough to lure almost anyone into trying. While fossil bones may not provide any grounds for such speculation, the artifacts created by humans may provide a basis for inference about some aspects of social life, particularly about division of labor, not between males and females, but within the group as a whole. If we come forward in time sufficiently, to periods in which humans produced many artifacts that have survived and have been unearthed, one can, I think, make some statements, that can be somewhat constrained and supported by data, concerning specialization of labor or the lack of it.

The specific issue on which we might make headway is this: we know that, say, 20,000 years ago humans manufactured from stone a variety of tools with sharp edges and points. The *technology* of making such tools is, in principle, simple enough so that with instruction we can be sure it was available to virtually anyone and, given the importance of these tools in the life of those people, we can well imagine that children started to learn how to make tools at quite early ages. At the same time that the technology is simple, its *execution* requires practice and considerable coordination and skill. While everyone did, undoubtedly, learn how to make such tools, there must have been considerable variation in the level of skill and competence achieved by different people. How, then, did they choose to organize their work? Did they rely on the most skillful member of the group to make the tools while the less skillful toolmakers did other things? Or did each person make all his tools for himelf, regardless of the level of skill he had attained? The issue applies, of course, not only to stone tool technology but to all the activities that were necessary or important in these people's lives.

If we regard the human being as a rational creature, one might expect that there would have been at least partial specialization of function in accordance with level of skill. If human groups organized their work to more efficiently exploit their environment, certainly the more skillful stone knapper would make the stone tools and the more skillful hunter would do the hunting. It would seem foolish for a skillful hunter to spend much of his time making his own inferior tools. To find consistent evidence of specialization by skill would, consequently, not be at all surprising. It is surprising, however, that one does not find such evidence. Although the indications are far from overwhelming, they point to a social organization without even partial specialization of function by level of skill, each person doing everything himself, each one making his own stone tools, for example. It is only much later, perhaps about 6,000 B.C., that one begins to find the kind of specialization of function that is so prevalent today.

What kind of evidence are we talking about? What, in the archaeological record, can be taken as indicating the presence or absence of specialization by skill? It turns out, naturally, that there are not many unequivocal indicators of specialization or of its absence. One seemingly good indicator would be the distribution of certain kinds of artifacts, such as the tools used to make other tools, throughout the site. For example, Mellaart (1975) describes the findings from excavations of Jeitun, dating back to about 5,500 B.C. in the Transcaspian lowlands, originally reported by V. M. Masson, in Russian, in 1970. The occupants of this village site, with permanent houses, grew domesticated wheat and barley, already had domesticated goats and sheep, and included sewing and weaving among their numerous activities. Tools that were found there included sickle blades made of stone set in bone hafts, awls and needles made of bone, stone adzes, and chisels for working wood.

According to Mellaart, "from the distribution of artifacts in the settlement it can be established that there was as yet no recognizable specialization of labour and according to the excavators each household made its own tools in the courtyards that were used as a working area" (1975:212). This kind of evidence sounds conclusive, but it is only conclusive about the specific site of Jeitun. As a general indicator it is a one-way street. The opposite kind of finding, namely, a concentration of toolmaking activities in one area of a village, does not provide evidence that specialization of function did exist. It merely provides evidence that common work areas existed.

Beidha, a site in the Jordan rift valley dating to about 6,500 B.C., and Çayönü Tepesi, in southwestern Turkey dating to about 7,000 B.C., provide good examples of such specialized work areas in very early villages. Kirkbride (1968) describes just such concentrations of activities in certain areas in Beidha. She reports finding one room that seems to have been devoted mainly to polishing stone, another devoted to working bone, another that seems to have been a place for butchering, for example. She herself interprets these working areas as providing "evidence to indicate some degree of craft specialization" (1968:268). Similarly, Braidwood et al. report uncovering a building in Çayönü Tepesi "made up of six or seven small rectangular rooms, each with its own characteristic yield of tools. It seems to have been a workshop utilizing mainly ground stone and bone implements" (1971:1239).

It is, of course, possible that Beidha and Çayönü Tepesi were relatively unusual places, showing beginnings of specialization by skill earlier than many other similar villages. But the evidence of specialized working areas is not good evidence for such an assertion. Indeed, the existence of specialized work areas is very common in towns and even in temporary campsites, and for good reason. Producing sharp stone tools, for example, leaves a considerable amount of debris, pieces of stone which also have sharp edges. Indeed, an unskilled worker will quickly acquire numerous scratches and cuts from this debris. It seems highly sensible to have such a working area away from other activities. The same kind of consideration would incline a group to have a separate area for butchering animals, although the nature of the debris is different. Other kinds of activities require very heavy equipment, not easily movable, and this, too, would lead to a concentration of such activities in one or two areas. It is certainly easy to imagine that anytime someone had a task to do, he would go to the appropriate area to do his work.

The only kind of archaeological evidence that I can think of that would be at all convincing with regard to specialization of function by skill in such very early communities is the uniformity, or lack thereof, in the quality of the artifacts uncovered. Assuming that there would be considerable variation in any particular skill among humans, an assumption that seems highly warranted, there would be considerable variation in the quality of manufactured items within

any community that did not practice specialization. Only if a particular craft was exclusively in the hands of those who were most skilled
would we find uniformity of quality—at a high level, of course.

Unfortunately for us, the archaeological reports of excavations rarely
make statements about the uniformity of quality of the manufactured
goods. The evidence is there but it exists in the minds of the archaeologists, not in print. Discussing the issue, for example, with
Professor Bar-Yosef and his colleagues, and looking at a large collection of stone tools from Natufian and Kebaran sites, it was apparent
that there was considerable variation in the quality of the tools and
in the skill with which they had been made. Perhaps the reason that
this kind of variation is not mentioned often in published accounts is
that it is the usual, expected thing and causes no particular notice.

One does, here and there, find occasional statements in the literature about this issue, almost always when the excavator is surprised
to discover uniform, excellent quality. One of these is especially val-
uable. Mellaart, who excavated Çatal Hüyük—an unusual place in
Anatolia which existed from about 6,500 B.C. to perhaps 5,800 B.C.—
reports as follows: "The amount of technological specialization at Çatal Huyuk is one of the most striking features. . . . The result of this
specialization is equally apparent, for the quality and refinement of
nearly everything made here is *without parallel in the contemporary
Near East*" (1967:211; italics added).

Clearly, there was specialization by skill in Çatal Hüyük. Equally
clearly, according to the knowledge possessed by Mellaart, such specialization was unusual, if not unique, for western Asia in the seventh millennium before the Christian era.

We are so accustomed to specialization of function, and the absence of such a practice seems so inefficient and irrational, that one
is tempted to question the weak evidence presented above. Why would
smart, ingenious, imaginative human beings not have chosen to benefit from having each task performed by the most skillful members
of the group? Do we have any strong, clear and unambiguous evidence that any human group, anywhere at any time, chose a form of
social organization in which everyone did everything?

In an attempt to answer the last question we can look at the social
organization and division of labor, outside of different tasks for men
and women, in modern groups that still live by hunting and gathering. Two cultural anthropologists that I asked about this issue both
assured me quickly that the prevalent practice in modern hunter-

gatherer groups is that "everyone makes his own tools." Trying to find the evidence for this in the published literature is, however, not so easy.

It is rather strange that most of the published reports about modern hunter-gatherer groups do not mention anything about this issue. In a book entirely devoted to such groups (Lee and DeVore 1968) there is not a single statement of relevance to specialization by skill although there are many mentions of specialization by sex. Here and there, fortunately, we do find an occasional statement. Lee, in his book about the !Kung, people who live by hunting and gathering in the Kalahari desert of southern Africa, provides a detailed description of each tool they use, how it is made, and whether it is a tool made by men or by women. In one instance he says, "Ironworking skill is generally distributed throughout the !Kung population, although a few men are acknowledged to be better at it than others" (1979:137). Another somewhat less direct comment may be found when he discusses a list of tools and says: "Column 1 shows the time in minutes required to make the item and indicates whether *the maker is the man or woman of the household*" (p. 272; italics added). The implications seem clear that among the !Kung there is no specialization, even partial, based on differences in skill.

A graphic description of this same kind of situation is provided by Vial concerning stone tool manufacture by Jimi natives of New Guinea:

> It took one man fifty or sixty blows before he got a suitable slab from the original block. He was sitting cross-legged with the block in front of him and soon his shins were bleeding from cuts by the flying fragments. The other operator, a much younger man, got a good slab quickly and, holding it in his left hand, began chipping it with a smaller round sphere of stone in his right hand, hitting it on the edges and chipping little pieces off. He had quite a good blade, seven inches long, chipped ready for polishing half an hour after arriving at the quarry. The process looked easy, as if anyone could do it. The older man was not so successful, taking longer to get a suitable slab, and having more difficulty in reducing it to the shape for polishing. (1940:159)

Vial goes on to say:

> According to my informants, all men of the villages in the area are able to make stone axes; the craft is not confined to a few

men. All the processes of manufacture are also carried through by the one man, and there is not specialization. (p. 160)

Such total absence of specialization is not universal, however. Among the Australian aborigines there are some clear references to specialization by skill. Berndt and Berndt report:

A few men here and there may have a reputation for being particularly expert in some task: building a canoe, making feathered string, preparing a dugong or turtle harpoon, and so on. They will expect some "payment" for their extra help in such matters, even if this is only a share of the meat caught with the harpoon or the fish carried in the canoe. This could almost be called craft specialization, but of a rather elementary kind. (1964:111)

Another example is mentioned by Allchin, discussing the manufacture of ground stone axes in central Australia. She writes that "the manufacture of such an axe was a specialist's task and the man who made it was recognized as an expert craftsman" (1956:119).

It is quite clear that not all modern groups that live by hunting and gathering abhor specialization of work on the basis of skill. On the other hand it is clear that some do, that some human groups find it congenial to have everyone manufacture his own tools—it is a possible form of social organization. It seems most consistent with the available evidence to conclude that before the seventh or eighth millennium B.C. there was a general absence of specialization in human groups.

Everyone will agree, however, that after some millennia have gone by, when we reach the period between 5,000 and 4,500 B.C. in western Asia, specialization by skill had become the normal thing. One of the earlier clear examples of this is reported by Mallowan and Cruikshank (1935). In excavating Arpachiyah, a town dating to about 5,000 B.C. in prehistoric Assyria, they found many workshops but they also report on the uniform excellence and elaborateness of the pottery, the jewelry, and the metalwork. There is no question about the prevalence of specialization in the following millennium. There is little to be gained by giving more examples.

We do not have to concern ourselves too much with questions of precisely when the earliest evidences of specialization appear. Whether the change occurred over a period of two thousand years or four thousand years is inconsequential for the point that a momentous change in social organization did occur. Prior to 8,000 B.C. man's technology, on which he was so dependent, was not in the hands of specialists, it was available to and practiced by all. However, in the settled, sedentary towns which came increasingly into being, by 4,000 B.C., many segments of this technology were in the possession of specialists. How and why did such a change occur? If a social organization involving specialists was congenial to humans one would expect to have seen evidence of such functioning from very early times. If it was not congenial, why did human groups increasingly embrace it?

The answer, I think, is that human groups did not embrace it: technological specialization was forced on them. Or, perhaps, it is more correct to say that, unwittingly, they forced it on themselves. Two major factors were primarily responsible—the growth of organized, long-distance trade and the almost unbelievable proliferation of new and different technologies.

How far back in human prehistory the beginnings of trade go is a matter for conjecture only. Casual trade between one small group coming into contact with another might go back a long time indeed. Organized, deliberate, long-distance trading is, however, of relatively recent origin—probably not older than 20,000 years ago, perhaps not older than 10,000 years ago. To positively identify such trade, one must rely on finding material in places that are far removed from the known source of that material. It also helps to conclude that organized trade existed if the material in question is highly desirable by humans and it, or its equivalents, are not accessible nearby.

The earliest evidence on which one could argue for long-distance trading is the frequent occurrence, in inland areas, of marine seashells used for ornamentation. There are sites in central and eastern Europe, for example, in which marine shells coming from both the Mediterranean and the Black Sea are widely found. The distances between the sources and the site locations are, not infrequently, in the neighborhood of 200 to 350 kilometers (Hahn, referred to by Phillips 1980:75). These sites probably date back to 20,000 years ago, perhaps even earlier. In many Kebaran sites of the Levant, dating back to about 17,000 years ago, marine shells from the Mediterranean are also found in inland areas (Bar-Yosef 1980). Some of these shells, in slightly later periods, may even have come from the Red Sea, somewhat farther away.

Although it is possible that these distances were traversed occasionally, or even regularly, by the migratory groups that lived then, it is by no means unlikely that the wide distribution of such shells was the result of organized trade by groups living in closer proximity to the seas. What may have been traded in return is anybody's guess, perhaps flint. But it seems certain that if this did represent long-distance trade, it involved exchange of raw materials and represented an extremely minor aspect of economic life.

By the time settled year-round communities had come into existence, it is clearer that long-distance organized, trade existed. Such organized trade may, indeed, have been facilitated by the existence of such communities since those who engaged in such trade knew exactly where to find the settlements year after year. Under such circumstances one can imagine the development of stable trade routes and, fortunately, it is even possible to partially reconstruct, today, some of those routes employed so long ago. This happens to be possible because of the unique characteristics of what was once a highly prized commodity, namely, obsidian.

Of all the possible materials for making flaked stone tools, the best is glass. Its fracture patterns are precise and maximally controllable. Obsidian, which is naturally occurring glass, produced under some circumstances by volcanic activity, was much sought after and highly prized for these characteristics. The sources of obsidian are not abundant; in some areas of the world they are rare indeed, and if one finds obsidian in such areas it must have been imported. In addition, the original source of any given piece of obsidian is almost always precisely identifiable because during its formation this natural glass is mixed with that unique set of mineral impurities that happened to be present at the local scene. Even obsidian that is produced at the same place, but in two different volcanic eruptions, can be distinguished. Sometimes there are difficulties in identifying the source if two sources of obsidian are somewhat similar or if there is a possibility of unknown sources that are not too far away. Most of the time the analyses of the impurities in the obsidian are definitive, however; we do know precisely where it came from.

Thus, there is clear evidence of traffic in obsidian between sources in central Anatolia and communities on the south coast of Turkey, which is on the other side of formidable mountains, the Taurus range, a traffic which dates back to at least 8,000 B.C. There is also clear documentation of the presence of Anatolian obsidian as far south as Jericho and Beidha between 7,500 and 6,500 B.C. It is not possible to doubt that this trade is organized and purposeful.

The most convincing evidence of early organized trade comes from farther west, from the Mediterranean. There is and was a major source of obsidian on Melos, an island that is now part of Greece. There is clear evidence, dated to about 7,000 B.C., of the presence of obsidian from Melos in the Franchthi Cave in the Peloponnese (Dixon 1976:298). This obsidian could not have moved gradually, traded many, many times by prople in local contact with eath other. This obsidian had to be purposely transported over a distance of 120 kilometers by sea. As an aside, this also represents the earliest solid evidence of sea traffic and seafaring skills.

This trade in obsidian is, however, in its beginning stages at these early times:

> Small amounts of obsidian . . . from Nemrut Dag by Lake Van [in eastern Turkey] began to reach the southern end of the Zagros foothills 800 km. from the source from the seventh millennium onward. . . . The proportion of [this] obsidian in the total chipped stone at Early Neolithic sites in the Zagros area drops off dramatically away from an obsidian-dominated "supply zone" within 300 km. of the postulated sources. . . . In later times [this] obsidian is found still further afield and the number of sources represented in material from one site tends to increase. (Dixon 1976:304)

Obviously, the trade grows. By about 4,000 B.C. there are ample supplies of obsidian from Lake Van in southern Mesopotamia, 1,500 kilometers away. And of course, sea trade in the Mediterranean grew and became increasingly economically important.

It is vital for our understanding of the impact of trade on social organization to consider what goods were given in exchange for this highly desirable obsidian. And on this point there is no evidence from the periods of very early trade. However, the exchange goods had to be things that others who lived elsewhere wanted that were locally unavailable to them. Perhaps cereal grains were traded to areas that did not have them; domesticated animals could have been highly desirable for some communities; wood may have been shipped to areas that had few trees—one could construct a long list of possibilities. It is my guess, however, that whatever it was, the very earliest trade was primarily one involving raw materials. And, to the extent to which this was true, such trade would have exerted only moderate pressure toward specialization by skill within any community, except insofar as the activity of voyaging and trading itself was concerned. There undoubtedly arose entire communities that specialized, in a sense. Obsidian quarrying, for example, could only occur at obsidian sources and communities near such sources could become specialists in that activity.

But trade in finished, manufactured goods probably did not lag too far behind trade in raw materials. A young person growing up near a source of obsidian would have had more opportunity to become very skillful at working that material than someone who only saw pieces obtained in trade; someone living in an area in which sheep produced very fine wool would likely become more knowledgeable and skillful about spinning that wool and weaving with it. The finished products developed and made by the communities close to the raw materials would have been finer and become desirable commodities for trading. And certainly we know that by 4,500 B.C. such trade in finished products was common.

Trade in manufactured products does, indeed, have a strong impact on the social organization within a community. Products made by highly skillful humans can be traded, not cruder products. There had to be a transition period, perhaps a long one, during which everyone in a community might still produce their own product for their own use, but only the more skillful would produce extra products that could be used in trade. But such a transition state is an unstable one. The person who spent much of his time making magnificent pottery did not have time to do other things. Specialization of function by skill had to become the general rule.

Perhaps even more important than trade, but not totally independent of it in its effects, was the rapid proliferation of technologies that occurred during this same period of time. Certainly, by 4,500 B.C., one person, no matter how talented, could not within one lifetime acquire all of the knowledge and skills necessary to manufacture all the things which humans had come to depend on for survival. There is no way to communicate this state of affairs except the painful one of enumerating the large variety. To spare the reader I will not be exhaustive. I will mention only enough of the major technological developments to make the point. What we all know is true today—no one can know and do but a small fraction of the things we depend on in our lives—was already true more than six thousand years ago. The fraction has simply become smaller and smaller.

By 6,500 B.C. ceramic pottery is found in many areas of western

Asia and by 4,500 B.C. it is a major industry. Pottery requires know-ing about and finding proper clay, knowing how to prepare the clay, how to fashion the pot and, what is most important, the ability to produce very high temperatures to fire the clay-finished pot into a serviceable durable, container. By 4,500 B.C. the potters wheel al-ready had been invented.

The earliest known use of copper, to my knowledge, dates to about 7,000 B.C. in Çayönü Tepesi, southeastern Turkey (Braidwood et al. 1971). Here they made some simple metal tools by cold-hammering native copper. By 4,500 B.C. the use of copper had become so wide-spread in western Asia that this is generally thought of as the begin-ning of the "Chalcolithic Period," meaning the age of copper and bronze. This use of metal did not just add one new isolated technol-ogy. In addition to working and fashioning the metal, there were also the technologies of mining and smelting the ore. The introduction of bronze, which required mixing of copper and tin, made the process even more complex.

The spinning of thread and the weaving of cloth, which may have started as early as 7,500 B.C., developed into a widespread textile in-dustry. Together with this, domestication of sheep introduced the new material of wool with its attendant technology; needles were made of bone for sewing; serviceable hand looms had to be invented and manufactured.

We have already mentioned the evidence for boats that made long voyages going back to 7,000 B.C. The technology of boat construction continued to develop and was far along by 4,500 B.C. The earliest drawings of boats, Egyptian and Sumerian, date back no further than about 3,500 B.C., but they represent already highly developed vessels.

We know that the earliest construction of permanent houses dates back to the first sedentary communities, about 9,000 B.C. Here, too, the technology became more complex. While the earliest houses were oval-shaped or round, by 7,000 B.C. they were square, and by 6,500 B.C. multichambered structures existed. Plaster had been invented and plastered walls and floors become more and more common. By 5,500 B.C. multistoried buildings were constructed in some places.

Food production introduced new necessary knowledge concerning planting in the proper season, storing food, breeding animals and, by 4,500 B.C., in Mesopotamia there were already the definite begin-nings of extensive artificial irrigation. And the old skills were still needed—humans still quarried and flaked stone for tools, leather was still worked, wild animals were still hunted, mats and baskets still woven, and so on.

Man's ingenuity, imagination, and inventiveness—a dominant characteristic for millions of years—had accumulated a body of knowledge and techniques that surpassed the capacity of any single human. Specialization of function was certainly forced on human groups. It is easy to view this accumulation of knowledge, this proliferation of technologies, as a marvelous accomplishment, which it is—one must marvel at it. More and more the environment had been controlled, and more and more the human lived in a world made by himself.

But all this had its consequences. Specialization of function produced a profound change in the structure of human society. The nature of relationships among persons, even if those relationships were still egalitarian, now involved a different degree of interdependence than was true in an era in which each person was more self-sufficient. We are not discussing cooperative relationships here. Cooperation among members of human groups must have existed for millions of years—cooperation in hunting, in protection from danger. And cooperative relationships undoubtedly continued. But specialization of function introduced dependency or, if your prefer, interdependency or mutual dependency—but dependency nevertheless.

Someone who worked primarily with metal or who devoted much time to producing pottery was dependent on others to supply the food needed to live. With the increasing importance of long distance trade, the people on whom one was dependent were not even always in one's own community. If, as we have conjectured in previous chapters, the human strives determinedly to control the world in which he lives, this reduction in self-sufficiency and the increasing distance away of some of those on whom one depended, would have produced uncomfortable psychological and social circumstances, circumstances with which humans still live today, even in enhanced form.

Specialization of function also introduces another aspect of social organization. While it does not force it, it opens a potentiality for differential status and power within a human community. Some functions might, from time to time, have seemed more indispensable than others and opportunities to acquire status and power would have existed. But status and power was not a new thing in human groups. As we will see in the next chapter, there was an area of human endeavor, which we have so far ignored, in which specialization had already existed for some time. By the period of about 4,500 B.C. most sedentary human communities were, almost certainly, already highly structured, stratified societies.

Which brings us to one final point. We have been describing changes that occurred in the settled towns of western Asia, towns which increased in number during these millennia. But, certainly, not all humans were living in such towns. It is impossible to assess relative proportions of population, but there were undoubtedly areas where humans still lived from hunting and gathering in small groups. It is also possible that some groups had already become pastoral nomads, moving from place to place with their domesticated animals and, as we know, both of these kinds of groups still exist in parts of the world today. I only want to point out that we have been talking about events, crucial ones it is true, that took place involving only some humans in western Asia. I have concentrated on western Asia because these things occurred there first, the data from there are the most plentiful, and what happened there determined the course of future events in the Western world.

Map 4 River Valleys. The great river valleys where the earliest "civilizations" developed.

CHAPTER TEN
Technology and Religion

M AN, that imaginative animal, had for many, many hundreds of thousands of years sought ways not only to exploit his environment, but also to control it, to change it at will, or to protect himself from it if he could not change it. He succeeded more and more, eventually, as we can see today, to an extent that is almost unbelievable. Consider some of the aspects of the environment that he was already able to control as long as twenty thousand years ago.

With the use of fire he was able to make the local temperature warm even when it was generally cold; he could illuminate a local area even in the dark of caves or of night; he was even able to change inedible material into edible food by cooking.

By inventing rafts and boats he was able to produce a new food, fish; he changed water from a barrier to movement into an easy means of movement.

By various kinds of construction he could protect himself from wind and rain—the local environment was made dry and calm even in the midst of a storm.

None of man's technologies for controlling the world were perfect—sometimes they failed. Fire would, on occasion, get out of control with disastrous consequences; constructed shelter could collapse or be washed away by flood; boats had accidents and water remained, as it even is today, a danger as well as an asset. Such failures and imperfections did not, of course, lessen man's reliance on technology nor his quest for new ways of controlling more things.

My image of man convinces me that he must have tried to control just about everything—and he still does. He undoubtedly tried to make it rain when it was too dry. (We are still trying and perhaps cloud seeding may one day be more effective.) He probably tried to make it locally cool if the weather was too hot. (It is only recently that he succeeded in producing effective air conditioners.) He certainly tried to ensure an adequate supply of game and plant food and, later, did bring these supplies more under his control through agriculture. It would be surprising if he had not tried to find ways to prevent floods (we now build levees and dams), to prevent earthquakes, to prevent volcanic eruptions, and the like.

Certainly, there is no essential difference between an attempt to make warmth when the climate is too cold and an attempt to produce rain when the climate is too arid. The thought processes are the same and are, in their essence, peculiarly human: the idea that it is possible to control the environment in which you live; the imaginative invention of ways in which it might be done; the ingenuity and persistence to put an idea into practice. To us, with hindsight, knowing the natural technologies that were available at the time, it is clear that 20,000 or 10,000 years ago man was unable to produce rain, prevent earthquakes, or to control any events of that nature. That does not mean, however, that he did not try and did not, at times, convince himself that he had succeeded. In whatever way he did it, it was all the same kind of technological endeavor—inventing ways to control the world in which he lived.

There were, indeed, differences in the reliability with which warmth and rain could be produced at will. In retrospect we can conceptualize a difference between these two technologies, making fire and making rain, but to him they were both technologies, uncertain at times, very effective at other times. Thus, in the same way that we recognize the discovery of how to make, use, and control fire as a highly important technological event, we must also recognize that the invention of a god who controlled rain, together with the invention of ways to influence that god, was an equally or, perhaps, even more important technological innovation.

The technology that involved "gods," let us call it religious technology, had broad, powerful implications. The natural technologies were relatively narrow in their application. Fire had specific uses but did not help point the way to the invention of more effective hunting techniques. The invention of a god that controlled rain, however, suggests the possibility of a god that controlled the sun, or of a god that controlled human fertility. Indeed, so general were the implications of this means of environmental control that natural and religious technology were thoroughly mixed together. Humans realized that gods could also help make the natural technologies considerably safer and more effective.

Actually, however, there are two essential differences between natural technology and religious technology that ultimately forced them further and further apart. For natural technologies there are a limited number of ways in which an objective can be achieved, some ways easier or more reliable than others. The more effective techniques spread and took over, and there was a convergence of practice over very wide areas. For religious technologies, however, there was a wide variety of possible gods to invent and an almost unlimited number of ways to propitiate and influence those gods, no particular practice being more effective than any other. Religious technological practices, consequently, diversify, and large differences are found within even small areas.

The other difference between the two technologies is, perhaps, even more important. Until relatively recent times all of the natural technologies were within reach of everyone. Any person could, and did, successfully use these technologies, with variations in skill to be sure. Religious technologies were different. Not everyone was able, if required, to effectively influence one or another god for a particular purpose. One person who, during some particular crisis, did effectively propitiate the proper god and produced rain, for example, would likely have acquired a lasting reputation for his expertise. The social and societal effects of this were considerable, and I will elaborate on them soon.

How long ago, and under what circumstances, did religious technology first make its appearance? This is difficult, if not impossible, to determine from the archaeological record. Archaeologists are fond of inferring the existence of religion if they find evidence of deliberate burials of humans, particularly if the burials have some standard feature about them, such as a directional orientation or a flexed position of the skeleton, in which the knees were bent and the legs pressed sharply up against the chest. If deliberate burial is evidence of religion, then we know that earliest religion goes back at least 60,000 years—the time in which Homo sapiens lived. Some even think there is evidence for religious burial practice going back to the time of the finds at Choukoutien, at least 400,000 years ago:

> Skulls and jaws are present in such large numbers that one is led to assume that they were carried there intentionally. Furthermore, in four of these the occipital part was raised by successive fractures, as if there had been an attempt to reach the brain. This suggests funeral rites of the type known as "two stage," which were still observed among the Buginese on the south coast of the Celebes, before their conversion to Islam in the eighteenth century. The body of the deceased was carried far

from the dwelling and left in the open, sheltered from beasts of prey. When the body had dried out the head could be detached easily, without the need even to cut the cervical vertebrae. (No vertebrae were found at Choukoutien.) The skull was then solemnly carried to the village, carefully washed and became a kind of protective divinity of the family of the deceased. Sometimes only the jaw was preserved and it was worn around the neck, suspended from a cord, like a medal. Acts of ritual anthropaphagy were associated with this cult; the occipital hole was enlarged with blows from a club on the base of the skull, then the brain was devoured by those who wished to assume the virtues and merits of the dead man . . . although we are not able to prove them, the conclusions that can be drawn from such comparisons are striking. Jaws and broken skulls reveal a funerary cult, the importance of which cannot be exaggerated. (Bergounious 1961:114)

Clearly, Bergounious is drawing his conclusions by analogies to contemporary or nearly contemporary human groups, a procedure that we have argued is not very convincing. However, speculations about ancestor worship and beliefs in the power of dead individuals by ancient man continually arise from attempts to explain practices such as decapitation and various other burial peculiarities. Thus, Maringer declares that prehistoric man "believed the dead to be capable of some action, both for good and for evil. He ascribed to them higher powers than those proper to the living. We may therefore assume that primitive man practiced a definite cult of the dead which included rites intended both to safeguard the living from the power of the dead and to obtain from the dead protection, favor and help for the tribe" (1960:20).

Such beliefs in the continued active existence of dead people and about the necessity to propitiate and influence them, if true, probably represent the earliest forms of religious technology. The dead ancestor with his exceptional powers were the earliest gods. There is, in the literature, a uniformity of conclusion in interpreting the data about burial and the treatment of dead bodies. Of course, this uniformity could arise because writers and thinkers have not worked hard to find other possible interpretations. But I do not think this is the case. Rather I think the universal agreement results from the difficulty of finding other interpretations that seem at all plausible.

Certainly, burial practices would not have had anything to do with health or hygienic practices before there were large, concentrated populations. It would have been easier, and healthier, to have simply removed corpses some distance from the living site and thrown them away. And why the bewildering variety of practices involving the dead? In some locations the dead were buried in such an extreme position of leg flexion that they most certainly had to be bound before burial (Harrold 1980). In some locations exhumation was systematically practiced. The corpse was exposed in a place where the flesh would be eaten away—presumably by vultures in Çatal Hüyük, for example (Mellaart 1967)—and the skeleton then reburied, frequently beneath the floor of the house in which the family lived. Such practices persisted in many areas. The Egyptian word sarcophagous, for example, literally means "flesh eater." The bones, after dessication, were replaced in burial urns.

In other locations the skull was detached from the remainder of the skeleton and given special treatment. In early Jericho, for example, skulls were plastered, painted, cowrie shells inserted for eyes, and placed in prominent positions (Kenyon 1957). There are locations where the directional orientation of the corpse seemed important, and places where burial together with red coloring matter was frequent. Of all the various manners of treating the dead, only cremation was absent from early on. In addition, one must take into account the growing practice of interring grave goods with the bodies—jewelry, tools, utensils, food. Solecki (1971) believes that even as long as 40,000 to 45,000 years ago the humans that lived in Shanidar Cave in the Zagros buried flowers with their dead.

How can one understand all this, the widespread, although variegated, special treatment of the dead? Could it have been a natural reaction of humans to grieve at the death of a loved one and a desire to somehow preserve something about that individual, or to make that individual happier in some afterlife? This too does not seem plausible. It hardly accounts for bound, flexed position burials, exhumation practices, or various other special treatments. In addition, one must remember that 20,000 or 10,000 or even 5,000 years ago people lived with death in a manner that industrial Western societies have forgotten. It is unlikely that more than 50 percent, if that many, of live births ever survived past the age of three or four—and yet one finds a dearth of child burials in the period from 12,000 to 4,000 years ago. And people did not live very long even if they reached maturity. It was a rarity if someone reached the ripe old age of forty or forty-five. Death must have been part of life. It seems to me likely that modern grief reactions are a late-coming, cultural introduction.

It is easy to reach the conclusion that special treatment of corpses was the result of a widespread belief in the continued potential for action, somehow, of dead people and in their heightened powers to affect events, both good and bad, over which the living had little or no control. The special treatments were attempts to restrain and/or propitiate the potentially dangerous, potentially helpful, dead person. These must have been the beginnings of the belief in "gods" and the start of religious technology. As an aside, it is interesting to consider that if these speculations are correct, the belief in an afterlife preceded religion.

Such a beginning of religious technology would have had weaknesses that would gradually have been corrected over many millennia. The major problems would have been the large number of potential gods, the lack of knowledge about which gods controlled which events, and the uncertainties about the relative power of these gods—which gods were important and which were not. Just as it took a long time to improve the techniques of making stone tools, it took time to improve the religious technology. If a disaster occurred, a flood or a food scarcity, whose ancestor was responsible? And who had the power to influence these dead people, and which practices were most effective? Indeed, if a disaster occurred, it may have been good evidence that a particular group's own practices were ineffective, or that its ancestors had less power than those of some other group that suffered less from whatever had occurred.

In this way one can imagine "gods" emerging from ancestors and a narrowing down of the number and variety of gods. The test of how powerful a god was and of how effectively one could influence that god would, of course, have been empirical verification, just as with natural technology. If it worked well to produce the desired result, its validity was demonstrated. One can readily see that the prevention of natural disasters could have been one of the major well-validated accomplishments of religious technology. If an unusually severe flood, for example, led to the adoption of new procedures to propitiate a different god, either newly invented or borrowed from some other group, these new techniques would have effectively prevented such severe floods for quite a long time.

The human desire to control events, together with man's ingenuity, would have produced, over time, a proven set of gods, each controlling various areas of concern. Such more formalized gods would, of course, no longer have been in the close personal relationship to people that existed when the gods were their own ancestors. But even when more formal pantheons existed, the beliefs in the powers of dead ancestors did not totally die out. These beliefs merged with the more formal religions. In ancient China, dating to the earliest writing about 1500 B.C., there is clear evidence of ancestor worship. In Egypt, of course, the divinity of the rulers came directly from their ancestors, the divine line carried through the female. Even today, religious Jews will visit the graves of their parents or grandparents to ask them to intercede for them with God.

What, exactly, were the social and societal implications of the differences between the religious and the natural technologies. In early times, say before 7,000 or 8,000 B.C., the natural technologies were all available to each person and, as we have discussed in chapter 9, were practiced by each person. Even those who were relatively untalented could still make fire, flake stone, gather food, and hunt; it may have taken such untalented persons longer, the end result may have been less adequate, but each one could and did do all these things. It seems highly likely, however, that the effective use of religious technology would not have been available to everyone. Not everyone would prove to be successful in influencing the appropriate god to produce rain or to make the next hunt very bountiful. During a time of food scarcity, for example, one can well imagine a number of people failing to influence one or another god to produce more food. One individual who, after his own appeals to some god, found the location of some game to hunt would have acquired a well-deserved reputation for expertise, perhaps a special relationship with that god. The lack of personal relationship between most people and the formalized god would be consistent with such wide differences in effectiveness. It was no longer a situation where some were more, and some less, talented. Rather, the facts were that some could, while others simply could not. In this kind of situation specialization of function was forced. To again make a hazardous comparison with modern simple groups, the practice of religious technology or the making of religious ceremonial objects is usually a specialized craft even when no other functions are specialized.

One cannot help but imagine that the status of expert in any aspect of religious technology would have been somewhat insecure in the early stages of the development of this technology. Someone who had demonstrated effective influence over the god that controlled fertility might very well fail the next time that he was called on to influence this same god. One can also imagine the explanations and modifications of procedure that would follow such failure. Later on, the status and qualifications of the experts would have become more adequately protected. The effective propitiation of a god by the expert may have come to require proper exercise of rites by many others; the elaboration of a pantheon of gods produced considerable overlapping of power and function within the pantheon. One failure by the expert might be inconclusive since the god one sought to influence might be temporarily in conflict with some other god. The gods in a pantheon were rarely always in harmony with each other. The specialist in religious technology was eventually, of course, seen to be stably possessed of his ability, an ability others relied heavily on and which conferred status and power on the expert. Religious technology probably presented the earliest basis for the beginning of social stratification. As we will see later, it is no accident that from the first evidence of the existence of rulers and ruled, the rulers are regarded as having divine powers.

Earlier, I discussed the purposes of religious technology, purposes that I have argued were no different than for natural technology. One would also, of course, like to know something about the specific practices involved and how they developed. Before the advent of written language, the major source from which we can hope to glean some knowledge about the specifics of religious technology is pictorial— paintings, engravings, sculptures. Some of the oldest of these, and the most famous, are the remarkable cave paintings in southern France and in Spain, some of which date back to about 30,000 years ago. Drawn usually in red outline, in some caves in black, frequently located in relatively inaccessible and totally dark parts of the caves, they show magnificent animals and hunting scenes, among other things. Needless to say, there have been numerous interpretations of these paintings, many scholars connecting them with religious practices.

Imputing particular meaning to such paintings, in the absence of detailed, independent knowledge of the general culture, beliefs, and ways of life is, however, only an exercise in imagination. There are too many interpretations possible.

There is, however, one suggestive, hard fact that does emerge from these paintings, and it has been frequently noted. Wenke, for example, in discussing the paintings from Lascaux Cave points out that "one of the many curious things about these and other Upper Paleolithic cave paintings is that while animals are depicted in very real, very representational terms, the figures of humans are either simple stick drawings or else weird half-humans, half-animals" (1980:211).

Maringer makes the same generalization. In Upper Paleolithic art, he says, "human representations are far fewer than those of animals. And what is more, they appear, by comparison, like the products of mere dabblers, or as grotesque distortions; the naturalness and vitality of the animal pictures are almost completely lacking" (1960:78).

Obviously, these artists from long ago were capable of superb representation, even conveying tension, movement, and realism. There can be no question that they could have done this for human figures as well as for animals. That they did not do so can only mean that there was some extra meaning to, or consequence of, realistic representation. It seems reasonable to infer that the creation of realistic images of a human, or perhaps of any animal, was known to have possible undesirable consequences for that human. Therefore, human figures in these paintings were represented symbolically or were disguised. These ancient people had discovered either that realistic animal images had some useful technological value or, alternatively, that realistic human images produced dangerous results.

Far more numerous than cave paintings are the clay figurines that began to make their appearance more than twenty thousand years ago and spread widely throughout Europe and western Asia. These figurines are generally taken to represent gods and to have had significance in religious practices and beliefs. Most of them are representations of animals. When there are "human" resemblances, one finds the same theme of distortion as we noted for the cave paintings. One of the oldest of these, found in Willendorf and dating back to, it is established, about 23,000 B.C., is a beautifully distorted standing figure of a mature woman with very exaggerated buttocks, hips, and breasts. The face, however, is nonexistent—totally blank. Many similar ones have been found and are widely interpreted as representing a "mother goddess" having something to do with encouraging fertility. The absence of face or stylized distortion of the head is one of the few constancies one finds in humanoid figures. Some "humanlike" figurines have discoid heads or very elongated heads or birdlike heads or any of a number of other distortions. Animals, as usual, are much more realistic.

Apart from this the prevalent impression is variety. This is quite clear in western Asia, for example, around the seventh and eighth millennia B.C. While many locations have no human male figurines, others, such as Tel Es-Sawwan, near Samarra, and Ali Kosh in the Del Luhran plain of what is now Iran, have figures with exaggerated phalluses. In some areas bulls and rams predominate and are presumed to have male sexual significance. In other areas it is primarily ibex and in still others wild boar. One cannot begin to describe the vast variety of figurines one finds. It is not possible to say with any confidence what the practical religious function of any of them were or, indeed, if all of them did have any such function whatsoever.

It is only with the appearance on the scene of temples and shrines clearly devoted to religious practices that we can begin to make plausible inferences about the roles of various gods and the practices used to propitiate them and keep them friendly. The earliest instance of what must have been a temple or shrine was uncovered at Beidha (Kirkbride 1968). About 45 meters east of the village itself were found three structures built at different times during the period from 7,000 to 6,500 B.C. Floors were paved with purposely broken pieces of stone; beneath the floors was "a thick layer of some iron compound, foreign to the whole region and therefore brought in specially and laid on purpose" (p. 273); very large slabs of sandstone were precisely positioned at several places within each structure. What is more, the structures were almost entirely clean. Considering the obvious amount of work that went into these structures and the absence of any hint of purpose leads the excavator to say that "the only conclusion to be drawn is that they had to do with some kind of religious observance" (p. 273). While these structures from Beidha tell us nothing about the content or form of the religious practices, they at least do reveal that some of these practices already required special places, special structures, perhaps even special practitioners.

We start to learn more from the excavations of Çatal Hüyük in Anatolia, dated to about 6,000 B.C., not very much later than Beidha (Mellaart 1967). Çatal Hüyük turns out to be a particularly early and rich source of information about the details of the practice of religious technology. In the course of the excavation more than fifty buildings were uncovered that were definitely religious shrines. Somewhat more than twice that number of buildings were dwelling places. Mellaart (1967) thinks that, by chance, they happen to to have excavated primarily that area of the village that was devoted to religious practices, hence containing so many shrines and the homes, perhaps, of the practitioner specialists, the priests and priestesses. In addition to the large number of shrines his conclusion that the area is devoted to such a specialized concern is supported by the fact that although there are plenty of tools, pots, figurines, and the like, there are no indications in the area of the manufacture of any of these things.

One interesting aspect of the shrines in Çatal Hüyük is what they reveal about uniformities in the religious practices. While the contents differed from shrine to shrine, wherever certain topics were involved specific conventions held:

> Scenes dealing with death are always placed on the east and north walls . . . . Scenes dealing with birth occupy the opposite west wall and bulls are found only on the north wall. . . . Animal heads associated with red-painted niches are always on the east wall but goddesses and bull and ram heads have no special place and may appear on any wall. (Mellaart 1967:104)

The evidence seems strong that these shrines were indeed devoted to the practical purposes of religion. One aspect of this evidence is reminiscent of the practice, in the caves of France and Spain from an earlier epoch, of paintings hidden in dark, difficult to reach, portions of the cave.

> That wall-paintings and plaster reliefs of goddesses and animal heads had a ritual significance and were not purely decorative . . . is shown very clearly by the fact that wall paintings were covered by layers of whitewash after they had served their ritual function and that plaster-reliefs were made ritually harmless by the obliteration of the face, hands, and feet when a shrine was abandoned. (Mellaart 1967:82)

In one extreme case a wall painting was covered with approximately twenty coats of white plaster (Mellaart 1962:65). In addition, there are numerous instances of red imprints of hands on the walls. Melaart says that "it seems that worshipers dipped a hand in red paint and left an imprint on the sacred image" (1967:83). It is possible that such hand imprints, as a means of assuring personal attention from the god, goes back very far. Such prints are also frequent on the cave paintings of France and Spain.

While some of these practices show continuity with the past, suggesting the slow, gradual development of the procedures, another kind of evidence in these shrines indicates continuity with practices that were prevalent in later times. Gifts to the gods are found in profusion. "In all shrines small deposits of grain, tools, . . . pots and bone utensils, a few animals bones . . . , bulls' horns, egg shells, gaming pieces, stamp seals, in fact any acceptable gift were found *in situ* as they had been deposited by the worshippers and perserved by the conflagrations in which many of those buildings had perished" (1967:78). Such gifts and offerings must have been a dominant means of propitiation of the gods.

Almost every one of the shrines in Çatal Hüyük had some distinctively different plaster reliefs and paintings and, on the basis of these differences one can say something about the specific religious purpose of that place. There are clearly different shrines devoted to hunting, to human fertility, to death, to abundance of food and even, perhaps, to protection from leopards. The people of this village had a well-developed, differentiated religious technology. And, of course, the areas of human existence toward which this technology was directed dealt with the variety of human pleasures and woes—good hunting, abundance of food, fertility, protection from danger.

It is of great importance that the effective use of these religious practices in Çatal Hüyük already required a special place and the participation or supervision or intercession of specialists. Indeed, if Mellaart is correct, a distinct portion of a city was set aside for them. And there are some suggestions that these specialists were treated differently when they died. Burials are found in houses as well as in shrines, but there are a number of sharp differences between the two. Red ocher burials, although few in number, occur "almost exclusively in shrines. . . . Two groups of objects, never found in houses but confined to burials in shrines . . . are mirrors of obsidian and bone belt-fasteners. . . . Fine flint daggers and spouted stone vessels also appear only as gifts in shrines or with male burials beneath shrines" (1967:207–8). It is not unlikely that religious specialists were the ones who had a particular, personal relationship with some god and, hence, were buried in the shrine with special favors.

We have speculated that the inevitable ascension of expert specialists in religious technology, an expertness that only few could attain, would form a basis for status and power differentials. Hints that this did occur in prehistoric times come from Hacilar, another village in Anatolia also excavated by Mellaart (1970b). A large building of Level

II of that excavation, dated as having lasted from about 5,400 to 5,250
B.C., is identified by the excavator as a shrine. This is the only building of Hacilar II that contained any burials. In general, the people of
Hacilar buried their dead in some undiscovered place away from the
town. The strategic location of this building with respect to the town's
water supply and the implications of this for power and authority are
recognized by the excavator:

> Its position, controlling the access to the only well, its size, and
> its graves suggest a public building of major importance. In the
> period concerned the idea of any authority other than a religious
> one can hardly be considered, and the building was therefore
> probably the main village shrine and the seat of the local author-
> ity, responsible for the welfare, both religious and economic, of
> the small society of Hacilar II. (p. 36)

One might not, however, want to overstate the case for centralized
power and authority in this connection. Hacilar II had at least one
other shrine in a different part of the town, so the power of religious
experts would at least have been somewhat diffused. It is possible to
imagine that as long as there was a very great diversity of gods with
different experts capable of influencing different ones, power and authority would not become too centralized.

By the fourth millennium B.C. shrines and temples had become
rather frequent, their structure becoming more and more elaborate
and, in some areas, multistoried. They are found throughout western
Asia, and Gimbutas (1974) provides excellent documentation of their
prevalence in Europe. But there is little to be gained by describing
them in much detail except, perhaps, to emphasize once more the
diversity of specifics from place to place. They do not provide us with
good information about, or fuller understanding of, the details of the
religious practices that were followed, the functions of these practices
or the status and power of the technical experts in charge of the
religion. To further our understanding, we must move forward in time
to the periods from which written records exist. It is only after the
advent of writing that we can resolve some of the uncertainties of
interpretation, although by no means all of them.

Thus, we must turn either to Sumer or to Egypt in the third millennium B.C. These two areas possessed the earliest written languages that are now well deciphered, both dating to about 3,000 B.C.
or even earlier. The recovered written record from Sumer is much

richer than the record from Egypt and, consequently, we will dwell primarily on Sumer. The Sumerians wrote on clay tablets, many hundreds of which have survived, while the Egyptians, unfortunately, wrote largely on papyrus, a very perishable medium.

Sumer, at the beginning of the third millennium, consisted of a number of loosely allied, constantly warring city-states in what is now southern Iraq. Each of the cities had its own principal god and a large, elaborate temple built for that god. The god in the temple was provided with food, clothing, and a variety of other offerings. Thus, for example, the main god in the city of Ur was Nanna, the moon god; in Lagash it was Ningirsu, the mother goddess; in Uruk it was Inanna, the goddess of fertility. Each god or goddess had a broad range of powers and all of the gods in the Sumerian pantheon, more than a hundred, were recognized and propitiated, as occasion warranted, in addition to the city's principal deity.

From the earliest written records it is clear that there was a close relationship between the gods and the rulers and, furthermore, an identity of the ruler and the priest. The person who could divine the wishes of the gods, who knew how to keep them friendly, who could propitiate and influence them, was the ruler of the city-state. The title of "en" was first used for both priest and city governor. The relation that developed later between the governor, the "ensi," and the priest is well summarized by Gadd: "it may be inferred that originally the *ensi* himself was the priest and that, even when the functions began to be distinguished, perhaps through delegation of religious duties, the priest was still the relative and sometimes the destined successor of the *ensi*" (1970:137).

Authority and power were closely linked to the ability to maintain good relationships with and to influence the gods. This ability was, undoubtedly, the source of power and once the positions of governor and priest-technician were not held by the same person, the potentiality for conflict naturally existed. By about 2,400 B.C. one finds evidence of this in the records, scant as they are. Written records exist for this period from the city of Lagash (Safar 1949). During the years that Lagash was ruled by Entemena, the high priest of the main deity, Ningirsu, was named Dudu. Dudu dedicated objects to himself and had monuments inscribed to himself, something only rulers should have done. He even got his name inserted in some of the royal texts.

Another, somewhat later, ruler of Lagash named Urukagina, instituted changes that are generally called reforms, but which principally reasserted his own direct, close connection with the god Ningirsu (Rosengarten 1959; Diakonoff 1958). The changes directed a return to the practices that Ningirsu had originally ordained, Urukagina proclaiming that he had a covenant with Ningirsu. Throughout the document there hovers the problem of potential conflict between the ruler and the priesthood.

The effectiveness of the priests in propitiating a god was, as for any technology, an empirical question and the outcome of wars among cities was a major piece of relevant evidence. Certainly, being defeated in war could only mean one of two things—either our own god was no longer friendly, a failure of the priesthood, or the other god was simply much more powerful than our god. Accordingly, the characteristics of the gods, the relative power of the gods, and the appropriate religious practices did not remain constant over time. Things were frequently changing in minor or major ways and the explanations of defeat in wars, the changing relations between humans and gods, and the shifting power structure within the pantheon are documented in many poems, myths, and laments. A lament over the destruction of Ur by the Elamites about 2,000 B.C. provides an example of concern that the deity, whose temple has been destroyed, has deserted them. Some of the lines from that lament give the flavor:

O Ningal, whose land has perished, how has your heart led you on!
After your city has been destroyed, how now can you exist!

How long, pray, will you stand aside in the city like an enemy?
O Mother Ningal, how long will you hurl challenges in the city like
    an enemy?
Although you are a queen beloved of her city, your city you have
    abandoned.

(Kramer 1963:142–44)

Shifts in power among the gods are illustrated by the legend of how the goddess Inanna visited the city of Eridu, stole the powers and attributes (*me* in Sumerian) of the god Enki, and brought them back to her own temple in Uruk, thus presumably increasing her own powers greatly. The Sumerian pantheon was very unstable in the power relations among the gods. Although in principle An was supposed to be preeminent, little is heard of him. Innana became more and more powerful over the centuries. The god Marduk, who was a virtual unknown during the third millennium, became one of the most powerful gods in the second millennium. One could go on.

Of particular interest is a poem on the exaltation of Innana because it can be tied closely to known historical events: its writing is established to have been in close proximity to those events, and the poem is known to have been very influential for long thereafter (Hallo and Van Dijk 1968). Sargon of Akkad was the first one to effectively subjugate the various Sumerian cities and to establish a long-lasting dominance over the region. From his time on references are no longer to Sumer alone but always to the kingdom of Sumer and Akkad. His own reign lasted from 2,371 to 2,316 B.C. but the dominance of Akkad over the entire region continued until 2,229 B.C.

The people of Akkad were Semitic, not Sumerian, and the chief deity of Akkad was Ishtar, a Semitic deity, who was not part of the Sumerian pantheon. Such a situation, naturally, created great instability in the Sumerian pantheon. It is noteworthy that there is no hint of any endeavor to impose the Akkadian gods on the Sumerians. Many gods existed together and events reflected their relative powers. An interesting merging and meshing occurred over a number of years, reflected in the writings of Princess Enheduanna, the daughter of Sargon, which stamped the religion of the region for many years to come. Sargon's daughter, after the conquest, became the high priestess of Nanna, the moon god, in the temple of Ur and, in addition, the high priestess of An, the god of heaven, in Uruk. She also personally identified herself with Inanna, to whom she wrote a cycle of hymns. The meshing of gods is well illustrated by the many other hymns both to temples of Sumer, with their gods, and to temples of Akkad, with different gods.

In Sargon's old age all or most of the cities rebelled against him, and together attacked the city of Akkad. Sargon won decisively, defeating the others and producing more evidence of what was already obvious—that Ishtar was more powerful than the Sumerian deities. In the hymn on the exaltation of Inanna, written soon after the crushing of the revolt, Enheduanna does three things. She declares Inanna to be supreme over An, transfers all the powers of Nanna to Inanna, and subtly begins the process (pursued more fully in later years) of creating an identity between Inanna and Ishtar. Once Inanna and Ishtar were one and the same, and more powerful than any other gods, some stability has been restored.

As with all technologies, the practical results justify the theory behind the technology. The outcome of a military campaign frequently provided clear-cut, practical results. Success in war established whose god was superior or whose techniques for influencing the gods were better. Thus, with conquest came the vindication of a principal god. When empires developed, as larger and larger areas of land were brought under a single domination by military conquest, there were large regions in which one principal god was accepted as obviously the most important and the most powerful among the many gods.

Although the specific content of religion in Egypt was radically different from that in western Asia, the dynamics of religious practices and of change in such practices were similar. The Egyptian pantheon bore no similarities to the Sumerian and later Babylonian pantheons, the division of functions and powers were different, the practices for propitiating gods were different; but again one observes the close relation between ruler and priest. The kings of ancient Egypt were themselves descendants from gods, the divine line of descent carried through the female. The instability of power relations within the pantheon was also similar. With each new Egyptian dynasty there was a radical change in which gods were the most powerful.

It is, perhaps, important to also briefly look at very ancient Chinese society because it developed, almost certainly, without contact with western Asia. There one finds the clearest instance of ancestor worship. The ancestors of the rulers were, of course, the most powerful gods, and the rulers possessed divinity. Naturally, the ancestral power structure changed with military conquest. It is interesting to note that the earliest Chinese writing that has so far been unearthed, dating back to only about 1400 B.C., is primarily concerned with priestly divinations in conjunction with proposed military operations.

Polytheism was very successful and quite functional for a religious technology: it enabled the technology to remain empirically rooted. If one god failed to accomplish what was sought, one could try to influence some other god. There could be differences of opinion about which god was more appropriate to influence for a particular personal desire, and different people, with the aid of different priests, could pursue their own best means of controlling events. If one region suffered drought while another had sufficient rain, the former could, and undoubtedly did, adopt some of the gods and practices of the more favorably treated region. If the technology worked, that was fine; if it didn't, one could try new things until one found a procedure that did, again, work. Perhaps it was a bit like trying to find an effective physician to treat an elusive illness—one tries one after another until the illness goes away.

But the eclectic embrace of a pantheon of gods carries with it the necessity of constant revision of the hierarchy within the pantheon. The relations among the gods can, and do, get very tangled. As societies became more complex, paradoxically, the pantheon had to become simpler. Its hierarchy had to be more sharply defined since many events had more general impact and could, frequently, only be controlled by the divine ruler of the state. Wars, with the consistent, overwhelming empirical evidence they offered, hastened the end of genuine polytheism.

By the beginning of the second millennium B.C. the belief system in Mesopotamia can no longer adequately be described as polytheistic. It is rather in an intermediate state which some characterize as "henotheism," a concept that the dictionary defines as the worship of one god, but not to the exclusion of other gods. The process that, in retrospect, seems like an inexorable progression toward monotheism, had already begun.

It is not possible to know how many times someone may have had the idea, or the conviction, that the chief god was really the only god. It is unlikely that such an idea arose only once. In the early second millennium B.C., for example, Amenhotep III attempted to impose a monotheistic system in Egypt, the sun god being designated as the only god. This attempt, which was continued by his successor, Ikhnaton, was never successful—the idea was not acceptable.

If and when anyone propounded such an idea, it must have been an extremely difficult one to sell. It flew in the face of the evidence. On numerous occasions various gods were known to have controlled events favorably, and military victories gave evidence of the authenticity of the current pantheon. It would also have presented a psychologically uncomfortable situation—with only one god there were no longer any choices and alternatives.

It is surprising, then, that the idea of only one god ever got off the ground, that it ever took hold of a group of people. It did take hold, of course, but only in very unusual circumstances, if we take the account in the Old Testament as history. It took hold among a relatively small collection of people recently uprooted from Egypt, where the gods had not particularly favored them, now wandering in the

Sinai desert, isolated from the major trends and belief systems of the time.

It is not surprising, however, that if such an idea took hold, it would be accompanied by foolproof, iron-clad guarantees and assurances. This one-and-only god had to have a special relationship to these people, and the means of maintaining this relationship had to be detailed. This all-powerful god promised the uprooted people land of their own and, even more importantly, guaranteed them military victory again and again. And the means of propitiating this god were spelled out in detail—it covered almost every aspect of daily existence. This god was also capable of, and ready to use, terrible retribution if his rules and regulations were violated.

Of course, it did not work out well. The endlessly guaranteed military victories were not forthcoming. The Hebrews were defeated by Babylonians, Persians, Greeks, Romans. They were in control of the land that they had been guaranteed by the god for only a pitifully small time. We cannot know how many abandoned this monotheistic belief system. It may have been many. But for others the combination of failure and a monotheism that deprived them of alternatives led to fanaticism. Since there were no alternative gods to turn to, the problem must lie in either or both of two places. First of all, there may be significant violations of the proper means of propitiating the god, and by the time of the Roman occupation of the area, the Hebrews were already divided into many, many sects, each with its own interpretation of the proper propitiatory procedures.

Second, and more importantly, into any monotheistic system there must be incorporated the belief that the immediate purposes and intentions of the one-and-only god are unknowable. Whatever happens is by the god's design, and the human must not waver in his belief or in his proper practices. And since the human can no longer control real events through the gods, the conditions of one's life after death are forced to bear a weightier responsibility. Whether or not such a system does, in the long run, suit the psychology of the human remains to be seen. Monotheism is still newly arrived on the scene.

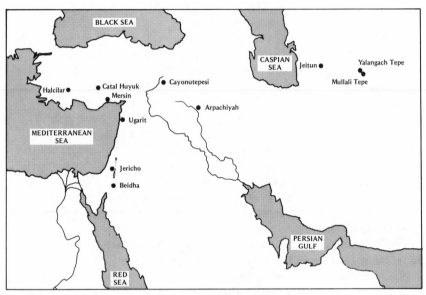

Map 5 Notable Cities. Some of the locations mentioned in these chapters.

CHAPTER ELEVEN
Fortifications and Wars

AT some point in the long history of our species humans began to kill one another, not only in isolated instances, not only as individual acts, but in an organized and purposeful manner. Naturally, there is uncertainty and controversy about how far into the distant past one can trace the beginnings of such organized killing, and there are differences of opinion as to how and why it started.

It is not informative to delve too far back into the past in an attempt to infer intentional killing from the condition of fossil bones. Even apart from the question of organized or individual action, one can say little or nothing about whether or not a human agency was involved in bringing about the death. In the 1950s, for example, many believed that fossil remains in southern Africa clearly indicated widespread internecine conflict and murder among the Australopithecines. Extensive analysis of this evidence, however, leads Brain (1981) to dismiss totally this idea of the "killer ape"; to him the evidence is much more consistent with the idea of predation by very large, now extinct, cats.

For anyone interested in the various interpretations possible from the shaky, ambiguous evidence, Roper (1969) has done an excellent job of bringing together and summarizing whatever data exist from the time of the very earliest human into the early periods of modern man's existence. From bones alone we cannot say much. One can sometimes determine whether an injury was inflicted before, at, or after death, but that does not tell us whether it was accidental or deliberate. More often than not, however, even a distinction between pre- and post-death injury to the bones is tenuous. The interpretations seem wholly determined by the predispositions of the interpreter. Almost any of the evidence can be, and is, interpreted in a wide variety of ways.

For the question of whether killing was carried out in organized, purposeful fashion, the evidence is even more useless. If we examine more recent instances in which it seems almost certain that the injury was not accidental, we still do not emerge with much knowledge about organized fighting and killing. An excellent example of this is reported by Solecki (1959, 1971). In Shanidar Cave he uncovered a number of rather well-preserved skeletons, one of which, skeleton number III, showed clear evidence that a blade had been stuck between two ribs. This did not cause the immediate death of the man since there was clear indication of partial healing of the bone before he died. The wound was of such a nature that it is highly unlikely that it could have been inflicted in any manner except that of another human being wielding the weapon. Solecki says that "Presumably, Shanidar III had been disabled *in a conflict with unfriendly neighbors* and was recuperating when he was killed by a rockfall" (1959:627; italics added). Why does such a suggested explanation arise—conflict with unfriendly neighbors? Perhaps he was wounded in a fight, in temporary anger, with his brother; perhaps a jealous woman stabbed him in his sleep; it might even, conceivably, have been an inadvertent stabbing during the confusion of a difficult hunt.

Another example that is interpreted by some as indicating large-scale organized conflict is reported by Wendorf (1968). In Nubia he uncovered a "graveyard" that was not associated with the remnants of any community or campsite in which people lived. The dating is uncertain and Wendorf refers to the period as "final paleolithic," putting it presumably somewhere between 8,000 and 20,000 years ago. This site contains skeletal remains of many individuals, many of whom were discovered to have stone flakes lodged in close proximity to one or another part of the skeletal structure. This raises the possibility that these people were killed by others, but many other intererepretations seem more likely. For one thing, many, if not most, of the remains show no sign of such possible injury with human tools. For another thing it seems highly unlikely that all the people buried there were interred at the same time. Rather, it may have been an area in which, over a long time, bodies were taken and disposed of to remove them from the area where the people lived. In reality, we cannot learn much from such instances.

We must move forward in time to those periods in which modern man could have produced other kinds of evidence which would allow us to do more than express uncertainty. One possible source of knowledge about organized killing is the later paintings in the caves of southern France and Spain and the more widespread drawings on rocks. If, say, in a painting or drawing dating back to fifteen thousand years ago, there was a portrayal of humans, with weapons, fighting each other, then we would feel confident in asserting that organized fighting existed at, or prior to, that time.

There are two caves in France, not too far distant from each other that do contain pictures that are relevant to the issue. In Pech Merle there is one human figure that is, perhaps, wounded by arrows. The figure, as is common with human depictions, is distorted or disguised. Breuil describes it as "a masked man with a pointed muzzle [who] seems to be pierced by arrows, unless he is carrying them" (1952:272). In three separate places in the cave at Cougnac there are figures of a human pierced with an arrow. Again the human figures are distorted, their faces resembling the beaks of ducks; in one of the figures the upper trunk and face are missing (Graziosi 1960).

In sum, unfortunately, the evidence is inconclusive. None of these are pictures that represent organized fighting. The context is quite different, and single individuals are portrayed. If they are representations of occurrences, why are the humans distorted with animal-like heads? Although it is possible that they represent enemies and the drawings are expressions of wish, hope, or magic, many other interpretations are possible also. Perhaps, they are an attempt, by magic, to prevent hunting accidents. Obviously, the absence of conclusive evidence from cave paintings does not mean too much. Perhaps warfare scenes were not popular, or perhaps caves were inappropriate places for such content. We must keep in mind, however, that scenes clearly depicting organized fighting do appear later.

The earliest known paintings that are described as representations of scenes of warfare are rock paintings from Spain (Phillips 1980:145). The dating of these rock paintings is quite uncertain. It was once thought that they were considerably older than recent evidence suggests. Pericot and Ripoll (1964), in their analysis of the evidence, conclude that the relevant period of naturalistic art lies between 8,000 and 5,000 B.C. Fortea (1975) suggests that this period began about 7,000 B.C. Up to now efforts to get dates based on analysis of the paints have not been productive. Organized, systematic warfare is a phenomenon of such magnitude, however, that one would expect it to leave other archaeological signs which could be interpreted with confidence. No such signs have been uncovered for this period in this area. If there were battles, they were not a widespread, frequent occurrence.

Organized killing, in raids or battles, does leave signs when it occurs, signs produced not only by the results of the warfare but also by preparation for it. Defensive preparations left major evidence for the existence of warfare, particularly the presence of defensive fortifications surrounding a town. Such fortifications take planning, time, and effort to construct. The reason for building them, never trivial, would be to protect the town from major, persistent threatened violence. Thus, if one finds fortifications in an area, particularly if such defensive practices become prevalent, one can say with some assurance that organized warfare, either for conquest or for raiding, already exists in that area. For our purposes, for attempting to understand the conditions that led to widespread wars and raids, it is important to locate and examine the area in which the earliest known fortifications existed.

It turns out that the earliest fortified, defended sites are found in western Asia and, so, we once more return to that area. If we can establish, with reasonable precision, the dates at which these fortifications came into existence, then there is the possibility of linking this development to other known changes that occurred in the region. We will, then, look carefully into the facts about the earliest known cities with walls. As we will see, in western Asia there exists a rather clear temporal dividing line between the period of no fortifications and the rapid spread of defensive structures.

Two walls existed in western Asia at least 1,500 years before any others, at Jericho about 8,000 B.C. and at Beidha about 7,000 B.C. The massive wall at Beidha, remains of which were found to be more than a meter high in places, has never been thought of as a defensive fortification. The reason for this is simple and compelling: there are steps on the *outside* of the wall providing easy access to the city. For defensive purposes that would have been ridiculous.

Then what was the wall for? Kirkbride comes to the astonishing interpretation, based on her belief that there had been no significant climatic changes in the area in the last 9,000 years, that the village was built on soft, shifting sand dunes, as exist today, and that the wall was erected "to consolidate their dune and prevent it from shifting" (1968:266). But why would people go to all the trouble of building a village in such an undesirable location? Another interpretation seems more plausible and reasonable. Beidha is built on the alluvial fan of a major wadi. These days the rainy season torrents bring mainly rocks down such wadis, but the climate around 7,000 B.C. was considerably wetter than it is today. The land had not yet suffered the denudation and resulting erosion that has produced the current barrenness. In that period of more rain and much more vegetation, the wadi carried, each year, new alluvial soil onto the floodplain. Thus, for example, there is an accumulated alluvial deposit, two meters thick, between the remains of Beidha and a previous Natufian occupation of the site. This, of course, is what had made the site attractive, the fertile, watered alluvial soil in which plant life fared very well at that time. The wall must have been built to protect the houses from the annual silting.

The wall at Jericho, however, has usually been thought of, following the interpretation of the excavator, as a defensive fortification. Kenyon says: "Somewhere about 8,000 B.C., Mesolithic hunters started to visit the spring of Jericho. Their descendants settled on the site and their occupation became increasingly permanent, until by 7,000 B.C. it had developed into a town with massive defences, covering an area of some ten acres (1960:100).

Only recently has anyone challenged this interpretation of the Jericho wall and tower and offered a different view (Bar-Yosef 1980). Bar-Yosef's contention is that the Jericho wall served precisely the same function, and was built for the same reason, as the Beidha wall.

Which of these conflicting interpretations is correct? The Jericho wall was, indeed, a massive structure, in places "more than two metres thick, and on the west side it is still preserved to a height of about 4 metres" (Dorell 1978:15). Inside the wall was a high tower, over nine meters in diameter at its summit. But the main evidence for this wall and tower having been built as fortifications seems to be simply that, in the absence of clear indication to the contrary, any wall is interpreted as defensive.

The issue, then seems to be how convincing are the facts that support the alternative view of the purpose for the Jericho wall. Bar-Yosef, in discussions about it, pointed out that a tower in connection with a wall to resist assault from enemies is invariably built on the outside of the wall. On the inside of the wall its usefulness in defense is seriously limited. On the other hand, at such an early period, the people of Jericho may not have been militarily sophisticated enough to know this. No one claims to have any reasonable guess about the function of this tower.

Of prime importance for interpreting the Jericho wall is the physical location of that ancient city. Not very far away from Beidha, the very old Jericho was also built in the middle of a floodplain onto which two major wadis annually poured new alluvial soil. If one visits the

site of ancient Jericho, it becomes very clear that silting of considerable amounts did occur in those times of more abundant rainfall. As
Bar-Yosef pointed out to me, the height of the old tower is not quite,
today, up to the height of the fields in that former alluvial fan. Since
no one imagines that, whatever its exact purpose, people would build
a high tower that overlooked nothing, it seems clear that the silting
of the fan on which Jericho was built continued for a long time. The
wall, whose thickest and highest portions face the hills from which
the wadis emerge, was probably constructed to protect the town itself
from the silting and was not a defensive fortification.

When walls that are truly defensive fortifications are found, they
are unmistakable, but no such fortifications have been found that are
older than about 5,500 B.C. Let us take a brief look around western
Asia to get an idea of when, in various regions, the first fortifications
are found.

In southern Turkestan the earliest walls are found in two cities
which were occupied in the period between 5,300 and 4,300 B.C.:
"Yalangach Tepe and Mullali Tepe are fortified with a wall, 0.5–1
meter thick, provided with round tower-like houses, regularly spaced"
(Mellaart 1970a;300; original references in Russian).

In coastal Syria the very earliest date might be about 4,500 B.C. in
Ras Shamra, known in ancient times as Ugarit: "Remarkable was the
discovery that traces of fortifications existed in these Halaf levels: a
solid, curved, and sloped rampart with a revetment of heavy stones
which appeared to have enclosed the northeast sector of the mound
at that early period" (Mallowan 1970:418). At the end of that phase
the evidence points to a violent invasion—the town of Ugarit was
sacked and burned.

In Anatolia, two cities are important to note because their occupation spans the time period from before to after the existence of fortifications. One of these is Mersin, the early levels of which were totally unfortified. The first fortifications at Mersin occur at Level XVI
dating to about 4,300 B.C. The Mersin fortress was attacked, the town
burned and the people killed (Gerstang 1953). The other site is Hacilar, which was occupied for two centuries about 7,000 B.C., deserted
for about a thousand years, and then reoccupied about 5,800 B.C.,
when a new village was built. This area, estimated to contain some
250 to 300 persons, was totally unfortified. By 5,400 B.C., however,
Hacilar had become a walled town and heaps of slingstones are found
at that level. It was burned and sacked about 5,250 B.C. Rebuilt with

exceptionally heavy fortifications, Hacilar survived another 150 years when it was again attacked successfully, destroyed, and the population massacred (Mellaart 1970b). It is perhaps interesting to note that the town of Çatal Hüyük, which existed from about 6,500 to 5,600 B.C., not far away from the location of Hacilar, never had any fortifications, nor was there any other indication of warfare (Mellaart 1967).

In other parts of western Asia—Iran, Iraq, Assyria—fortifications were absent in the fifth and sixth millennia B.C. Not until the fourth millennium have fortifications become prevalent everywheres. Once we find fortifications we also find clear evidence of warfare, burning of cities, and killing of people. If such warfare had been present previously, in the region, one would imagine that some evidence of it would have been located. During the period in the prehistory of western Asia from about 5,500 to about 3,500 B.C. raids, warfare, and destruction began, increased and spread widely. After about 3,500 B.C. warfare was continual.

Why did it begin? What produced this phenomenon that became so popular eventually? There can, of course, be a multiplicity of reasons, and the factors that were responsible for the onset of organized fighting might be different from those that helped it continue and spread. Bearing in mind all of these uncertainties and complications, it still seems worthwhile to see if any plausible basis for the onset of warfare can be discerned. Obviously, we do not want to attribute it to any of a variety of possible base human characteristics since, for many, many thousands of years, while conflicts and fighting may have occurred, human groups lived and flourished without warfare. We must, then look to the conditions of that time, what other things were happening when warfare started and spread, in order to try to establish some believable basis. It will all remain as speculation and guess, of course, but there is at least one process, coincident in time with the spread of fortifications, that can guide some of our guesses.

Defensive, fortified walls around towns appeared in the period following the spread and intensification of agriculture, the increasingly major reliance on growing domestic plants and husbanding domestic animals. In eastern Europe, for example, where agricultural practices were established about 2,000 years later than in western Asia, the earliest fortified towns date back only to about 3,500 B.C. (Phillips 1980). Could there be a connection between these practices, between intensive agriculture and warfare?

Let us remember that although the archaeological record of these millennia speaks mainly of villages and towns, the entire human population had not settled down to year-round occupation of one place. The villages and towns are easier for the archaeologist to find: centuries of occupation in one place leave identifiable mounds which can be spotted and excavated. In addition, the development of towns and the development of agriculture were momentous processes that determined much of the future of mankind. Naturally, these things capture the imagination of the archaeologist. We have no way whatsoever of estimating what proportion of the population was still seasonally mobile, still primarily or entirely dependent on hunting and gathering in, say, the fifth millennium B.C. We can be sure, however, that such groups did exist in western Asia at that time. Indeed, such groups still exist today in many parts of the world.

Why some groups continued to be mobile and continued to live off wild plants and animals is an interesting, unanswered question that need not concern us too much here. Perhaps they did not find locations favorable enough to permit them to settle down; perhaps their agricultural experiments were failures too often; perhaps they had developed other social and communal practices that militated against settling in one place. Whatever the reason, these mobile groups continued to exist, in dwindling numbers as the millennia passed, but they existed.

We have, in previous chapters, discussed at length the incompatibility between domestic and wild varieties of the same plant or animal. The wild variety, in the presence of domestication, becomes a weed or a threat. Wild food plants and wild animals did not flourish in the vicinity of communities that engaged in agriculture. But clearly, the incompatibility between the wild and domestic variety of the same food source produced, without intent and without malice, an equivalent incompatibility between two ways of life, between the agricultural, sedentary communities and the groups that hunted wild animals and collected wild food plants. The agriculturalists were inadvertently exterminating the food sources of the hunters and gatherers. These two different life styles could not exist in the same general vicinity. And as settled agricultural communities grew in numbers, as they did in the fourth and fifth millennia B.C., these problems also grew in extent and severity.

The archaeological record tells us little or nothing about what happened to groups that continued to depend on wild food supplies as those food sources became scarce. There were, undoubtedly, migrations to areas, distant from agricultural settlements, in which food was more easily obtainable. Some groups may have felt themselves forced to turn away from their previous mode of living and also to resort to agriculture in order to survive. Still other human groups, reluctant to abandon their way of life and unwilling to leave the territories they regarded as their own, easily came to regard the herds of domesticated animals and the stored cereal grains of the agricultural communities as possible supplementary food sources.

It is not hard to imagine that, gradually, hunting parties were transformed into raiding parties. The response of the settled agricultural communities to protect their supplies of food and other goods is not difficult to envision—walls to keep the raiders out and weapons with which to repel them. It would be rash to claim that this incompatibility between two different life styles was the only progenitor of what in time became the honored practice of war. Other kinds of conflicts could, from time to time, have arisen between groups that occasionally may have produced organized fighting. In addition, factors which later on facilitated the continuation of warfare might have existed on a small local scale much earlier. But the incompatibility at that time between the hunter-gatherers and the agriculturalists was intrinsic and must have been a major factor. And the coincidence in time cannot be ignored—walls around towns closely followed the intensification of agricultural practices.

The settled communities, in the long run, were bound to win. For one thing, as we have seen, their numbers were, locally, larger—they had higher rates of live births. Once they built effective walls they must have more or less adequately repelled most raids. If, however, a raid did succeed here and there, it could have been catastrophic. It is clear that it was raids that were going on, not conquest, as became the prevalent form later on. The earliest incidents of sacking and burning of towns show that the raiders did not come to occupy or control or rule—they came to take what they wanted and then left. The town then had to be rebuilt, preferably with stronger fortifications.

This was not the pattern of later warfare. By about 3,000 B.C. in Mesopotamia, for example, we find more or less continual warfare among settled, agriculturally dependent, cities. Clearly, the conditions that originated organized war were different from the conditions that sustained and nurtured it. Once an institution is established in a society, particularly a powerful one, it does not disappear easily, even if its original function has disappeared. The beginnings of organized fighting did create a powerful institution, warriors under the leadership of the ruler. Such an instrument could be used for a large variety of purposes. In time, the use of military power became an ordinary, accepted and honorable part of human existence.

With greater reliance on agriculture, suitable land to sustain growing populations became relatively scarce. The larger the scale of the agricultural enterprise, the fewer were the locations where it could be effectively practiced. When humans had to turn to artificial irrigation, the amount of suitable land area shrank even further. Only the great river valleys could support large-scale irrigation to feed large populations and control over such land, with the aid of military action, was certainly desirable. It is no accident that the earliest large-scale societies, maintained by military might, appeared along the great rivers of Egypt, Mesopotamia, India, and China.

It has been my intention here to argue that organized war is of rather recent origin and to provide a plausible account of some of the reasons that it started. Once begun, it had many ramifications and quickly became multipurpose. I do not intend to examine how warfare later evolved except to say that apart from control of land it also provided a means of protecting trade routes, acquiring an organized labor force, and accumulating wealth. This new invention of human society—warfare—became so integral a part of human existence that western Asia was continually involved in wars until the Roman conquest. It was only after understanding the ceaseless prevalence of war in this region for at least 3,500 years that I understood the full meaning of the Pax Romana—three hundred years of imposed peace.

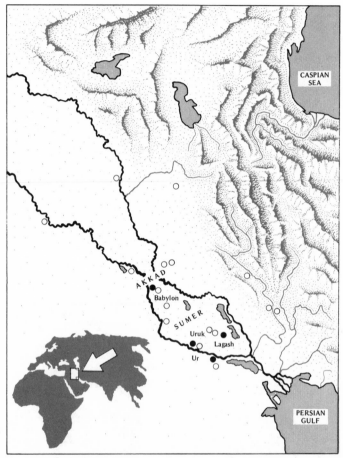

Map 6 Sumer and Akkad. The black circles represent some of the principal cities of Sumer. The open circles represent other locations in Sumer, Akkad, and a few in Elam.

CHAPTER TWELVE
Organized Societies and Human Slavery

THE steady growth in the size of human communities, the proliferation of technologies, the increased prevalence of organized fighting, and the general reliance on food production aided by irrigation pushed strongly toward highly structured, organized societies. All these factors also increased the need for an organized work force. How was this work force provided? The answer seems to be, at least in part, by capturing other humans and enslaving them. More than a century ago Blake wrote an impressive book on the history of slavery—impressive for its time. Early in the book he makes a statement that is startling to a naive twentieth-century mind: "It is certainly a curious fact, that so far as we can trace back the history of the human race, we discover the existence of slavery" (1858:2).

Five thousand years ago we already had highly developed societies which, while technologically less evolved than today, were quite mature artistically, ethically, and morally. It is true, however, that their ethics and their morality were different from ours today. Ethics and morality change rapidly; basic underlying biology changes slowly.

Is it true that human slavery was ubiquitous or, perhaps, did it only exist when and where special circumstances facilitated or forced it? In the hundred and twenty odd years since Blake wrote there has been much new excavation, many more discoveries of early written documents, and considerable advance in the deciphering of ancient writing. We now have much more information on the subject and another look is well worthwhile.

First, a word about the nature of the evidence and the meaning of a phrase such as "so far as we can trace back the history of the human race." In the absence of deciphered written records one cannot have any firm indication of whether or not human slavery was practiced. Paintings or engravings of people engaged in work are, obviously, no evidence; pictures of captives or prisoners with, perhaps, hands bound, guarded by armed men are similarly ambiguous: they do not indicate human slavery rather than captivity or punishment for crimes. It is only the written record that can tell us if humans were held as property, bought and sold, and expected to perform their assigned work, much as we expect a hunting dog that we have purchased to perform properly and unquestioningly during the hunt.

The history of slavery is, then, inherently confined to the period included in the conventional meaning of the word "history," beginning with the advent of writing. Before that is prehistory, about which we can only speculate—and will. For the purposes of examining early societies it is unfortunate that history dawns at widely different times in different places. As we already know, the earliest deciphered written languages are from Sumer, a loose collection of city-states in the Tigris and Euphrates valleys in what is now southern Iraq, and also from Egypt. In both these places written language appears about 3,000 B.C.

Many Sumerian clay tablets have been found, and much is known, consequently, of that society in the third millennium B.C. What is known about Egyptian society in this early period comes mainly from the occasional writings on stone—usually accolades to the accomplishments of important individuals.

Of the very extensive society in the Indus valley of India during this time we know nothing historically. There has not been uncovered any decipherable written language. The later Indo-Europeans who arrived in India during the second millennium B.C. also had no written language. But they did transmit accounts of their customs, beliefs, and history from generation to generation orally. It was not until about 800 B.C. that these accounts, the Vedas, were written in Sanskrit. In China the earliest discovered writing dates back only to about 1500 B.C., and discoveries to date are primarily divinations, oracle inscriptions on turtle shells.

When we look back, then, we are looking back unevenly, both in time and in scope. One can say though that Blake was correct, wherever and whenever one can look there were in existence well organized, highly stratified societies with the institution of human slavery well entrenched.

Of very ancient Egypt, prior to about 2,500 B.C., we know very little indeed. Nevertheless, even the scanty evidence argues that human slavery existed. Probably only members of the highest class of Egyptian society owned slaves. Representations in the tombs of the Old Empire show the great men of the kingdom and their priestly offices and the crowds of laborers who are, most probably, slaves belonging to the great man. In these representations, according to one authority, there are no instances of free peasants, artisans, or shopmen (Erman 1894). There undoubtedly were many such in the society but, presumably, since they were not the property of the great man, they were not represented in the tombs.

More convincing, perhaps, is a poem of very ancient origin (date uncertain) that speaks of a weaver who "must always sit at home at his work, and if he wishes to get a little fresh air, he must bribe the porter" (Erman 1894:101). By the XII dynasty (perhaps about 2,000 B.C.) there is more evidence that makes it abundantly clear that, by that time, even more modest households had slaves, both male and female, as servants.

In the second millennium B.C. descriptions in writing become more numerous. During the reign of Ramses III it is clear that slaves were property, just as land or cattle. The names of slaves were entered in official registers and slaves were branded with an official seal. "These slaves were despised by the scribes who said they were without *heart,* i.e., without understanding, and that therefore they had to be driven with a stick like cattle" (p. 128). These slaves were prisoners of war and those captured in raids. And they must have been appreciable in number. Ramses III at his death left a list of things he had done for the temples of Egypt during his reign. This preserved papyrus document lists, among other things, gifts to various places of worship of 113,433 slaves. It is difficult to know how much to allow for exaggeration in the interest of self-enhancement, but the numbers were certainly large.

In ancient China reliable knowledge about slavery begins only with the Shang dynasty, starting about 1500 B.C. In the *Book of Historical Records,* written during the Western Han period, which corresponds in time to about the beginning of the Christian era, there are references to still earlier times. It states that in the Hsia period, perhaps about 1850 B.C., war captives were enslaved. It also states that in the still older, almost legendary, period of the Three Dynasties slavery in China did not exist. It is, of course, doubtful that one can take as factual such statements made two thousands years later in the context of a society in which slavery had grown to very troublesome proportions.

The first written contemporary evidence comes from oracle texts of the Shang dynasty, and even here there have been some differences of opinion. Kuo Mo-go (p. 306, referred to by Ping-ti Ho 1975) interpreted the *chung* (literally the multitudes), frequently referred to in the oracle texts, as slaves and, hence, argued that the Shang dynasty, which lasted from about 1700 to 1100 B.C., was a thoroughgoing slave society. Ho argues against this, presenting convincing evidence that the *chung* were not slaves but simply the multitude of workers and peasants. However, he goes on to say:

> That the Shang was not a slave society does not mean that slaves did not exist in Shang times. Both oracle texts and archeological finds confirm the existence of scattered groups of slaves. . . . The majority of slaves, both of the royal household and those used for human sacrifice, seem to have been war captives. (1975:308–9)

> Significantly, the largest single category of slaves was the Ch'iang, a non-Chinese people of southwestern Shansi and parts of Shensi. Ch'iang in a narrow sense probably meant proto-Tibetans, but broadly used it meant all the non-Chinese peoples northwest of the Shang Kingdom. Large numbers of Ch'iang war captives were used as slaves in royal households, as horse grooms, occasionally as agricultural workers and auxiliary soldiers. (p. 310)

There is no disagreement and no controversy about the fact that such human slavery did exist. The only disagreements concern how widespread the use of slaves was during this period.

According to Ho (1975) there was no generic word for slave in the oracle texts of the Shang dynasty. In the period of the Chou dynasty (Western) which lasted from about 1100 to about 800 B.C., there was such a word and the written sign for the slaves meant, literally, "barbarian tribes."

By this time the extent of slavery had certainly become considerable. Two inscriptions on bronze vessels are given below to illustrate:

Document 1: Inscription on bronze vessel:
The emperor defeated the fiefdom of Chia and subjugated its lord. The lord of Chia sent tributes to the emperor to indicate complete submission and loyalty to the Chou emperor in future. The gifts are listed: ten high-ranking warrior families; one hundred slaves.

Document 2: Inscription on bronze vessel:
In the ninth month, the Chou emperor summoned Men [one of his ministers]. In the years of my ancestors some of my ministers served

the Chou house well. I shall act in accordance to the justice of my
forefathers and give them their due rewards.
Chon Nan Kung will be named lord and given land and people.
He shall also have the privilege of wearing the sash and regalia
of high honor.
Yeh Pan Shih will be given four administration officials, six
hundred slaves, fifty servants, and nine farm laborers.
Yi Shih Wang will be given ten attendants, three administration
officials, one thousand slaves, and fifty farm laborers.
Carry out these instructions speedily and see that these men of
high honor receive their rewards.

(private translation)

The practice of human slavery continued to flourish and became
more and more important in the functioning of the Chinese society
as the centuries unfolded. By the time of the Han dynasty, sufficient
records exist to make the picture very clear: China had become, indeed, a slave society in the full meaning of that phrase (Wilbur 1943).

Along the Indus valley of India a highly organized society existed
about 3,000 B.C. and probably earlier. At least two large cities existed
then: Mohengo-daro on the Indus River and Harappa on the banks
of the Ravi River. Artifacts found in these two cities together with
those found in Egypt and in Sumer provide unequivocal evidence of
contact and trade between all three of these organized societies. A
large number of seals have been uncovered in the cities of Harappa
society that have "writing" on them. Unfortunately, it is a proto-writing, entirely pictographic rather than phonological. None of the writing has ever been deciphered. About issues such as slavery, then, we
know nothing.

Sometime during the first half of the second millennium B.C. these
cities were destroyed by the invading Indo-European people, the Aryans. The language of these people was Sanskrit and they did leave
verbal records of their society, culture, and religion. The oldest of
these records is the *Rig-Veda* which, while being primarily an account of religious beliefs and practices, also conveys the history from
the early invasions up to about 1500 B.C.

The *Rig Veda* tells us that the Aryan advance into India was
very strenuously resisted. . . . The Aryans describe their enemies as dark in complexion, noseless or flat-nosed, of harsh
speech, not honoring the Aryan gods, not observing the Aryan
religious ritual, but rich in material possessions and living in for-

tified cities. . . . The Aryan invaders finally triumphed over the non-Aryans, many of whom were killed, enslaved, or driven further inland. (Gokhale 1952:22)

According to Gokhale the *Rig-Veda* describes the Aryan society as divided into three classes: the warrior-administrator, the priest, and the agriculturalist-artisan. "The slaves taken from the vanquished non-Aryan population performed all the low and menial tasks in the service of the victors" (p. 24).

It is clear, once again, that human slavery was practiced from the earliest times we can know about. The *Rig-Veda* is replete with references to human slavery and many of these are specifically references by Chattopadhyay (1970:4–6). And once more we see that it is war captives, both male and female, who are enslaved. It is interesting to note the early word for slave. "The people whom the Rigvedic Aryans fought are referred to as Dasa and Asura. These two are distinct, although later both are often referred to as Dasa, meaning thereby a slave" (p. 6).

We have saved ancient Sumer for last because it is the best documented: copious written records go back earlier than from any other society. Indeed, the earliest written indication from which one might make a fair inference of the existence of slavery dates back to the late Jamdat Nasr period of Mesopotamia, perhaps as early as 3,200 B.C. In the excavations at Ur conducted by Wooley (1954) about 400 tablets were uncovered from a strata indicating that they belonged to this period. The writing is not yet the familiar cuneiform but is primarily still pictographic. These tablets represent a late stage in the system of proto-writing from which Sumerian cuneiform written language developed. As one might expect, the vast majority of the tablets are records of commercial transactions. Most are "lists of cereals and products of cereals (flour, bread, beer, etc.) and of livestock; seventy deal with landed property; four are lists of men's names and about twenty are school texts, some of which give lists of gods; and numerous temples are mentioned" (Wooley 1954:46).

The question is: what are four lists of men's names doing among these tablets? Of course, it is possible that they were lists of school teachers or lists of merchants. But, in the context of so many records of commercial transactions it is also possible, indeed more likely, that these four tablets also represent such commercial transactions—the sale of human slaves.

There is further and more solid, evidence dating back to about 3,000 B.C. The earliest sign for a slave in the Sumerian writing was a composite of the sign for male (or female) and the sign for *kur,* which meant both mountain and country and, hence, meant foreign country to the lowland Sumerians:

> In fact, the term *kur* never applied to their own country but became gradually the generic word for any foreign country. We can thus conclude from the philological evidence that the earliest notion of "slave" was incorporated with the idea of "foreigner." It is logical to assume from this that some of the earliest—if not the first—slaves were captives of war and punitive raids. (Siegel 1947:9)

Tablets containing the signs for male and female slaves have been recovered in excavations at Fara and at Uruk and are generally agreed to date to about 3,000 B.C.

It is not until the Third dynasty of Ur, about 2,100 or 2,200 B.C. that there is considerable information about the practices and laws governing human slavery, but by this time the practices had already undergone considerable change. We will return to these later periods. But, for now, let us examine some of the characteristics of the earliest institutions of slavery, and speculate some about its origins.

At the earliest periods that we can talk about, all four of the major societies that have been discussed showed marked similarities in regard to human slavery. First of all, it was practiced, accepted, and had undoubtedly been going on for centuries before the times that we were able to examine. Second, the slaves, both male and female, were foreigners, captured in war or in punitive raids. Indeed, the word for foreigner became the word for slave in both Sumer and India. In China there was no very early general word for slave, but the word *Ch'iang* came to be generalized to mean non-Chinese foreigner, and these were the vast majority, if not the entirety, of those enslaved.

Such semantic changes are revealing. They occur even in relatively modern times. After the effective collapse of the Roman empire there was a period in which slavery in Europe was a relatively rare phenomenon—there were very few captives to enslave. The only captives were those taken in the sporadic battles on the eastern borders with Slavic peoples. The Roman word for slave, *servus,* meanwhile had changed its meaning to *serf* and later to *servant.* The word for the newly enslaved people, *Slav,* became the general word for slave.

At the earliest times there is no indication whatsoever that anyone but foreigners were enslaved. Indeed, the overall impression is of a sharp distinction between in-group and out-group. The latter represented the potential supply of slaves. As we shall see, this sharp distinction was breached in later times and laws came into existence to maintain at least partial prohibitions on the enslavement of the in-group. Only in China did the distinction eventually break down entirely.

How did human slavery start and why did it start? It is almost unimaginable that human slavery existed during the long period of time in which humans lived in very small groups, existing by means of hunting wild animals and gathering wild plants, moving their camps from time to time as seasons changed or as food in one area grew scarce. What would slaves have done then? How would they have been supervised and constrained? Why would they have been needed?

It seems reasonable to imagine that only after human groups became sedentary, only after heavy reliance on domestic grain crops and domestic animals created a need for an organized work force, only after stratification of society was rather well developed bringing with it a place for domestic servants for the powerful ones, only then might human slavery have been seen as a useful, productive device.

But all of that would still not have been enough. The idea had to occur to someone that one could capture another human and physically force that person to perform work that needed to be done. This ingenious idea had, of course, already occurred to man much earlier than when slavery might have begun. Indeed, the hunter-gatherers produced the idea.

Davis and Valla (1978), for example, have clearly demonstrated that the dog was domesticated in southwest Asia as long as 12,000 years ago. Someone, or some group, had had the remarkable idea that one could capture an animal, train it, and use it to help hunt and kill other animals needed for food. Whether this endeavor was easy or difficult to accomplish, and how it was accomplished, does not concern us here. The important thing was that human creativity and ingenuity produced the idea. And it was very effective. Dogs are very helpful in hunting. Even today, among contemporary hunter-gatherer groups, a hunter with dogs brings home much more meat than a hunter without dogs (Lee 1979).

Extensions of this idea must, of course, have come easily. Later on, other animals were used for motor power, transportation, and other kinds of work. The extension of the idea to humans was, undoubt-edly, also not difficult. To regard an enemy, a foreigner, a person who looked different and lived in a different manner, as a suitable subject for capture, ownership, and work, in short for what we now call hu-man slavery, was a thought that must have occurred to many in widely separated areas of the inhabited world. To the extent that the origins of human slavery represented a mere extension of the prac-tice of using animals to do work, it implies a clear, sharp distinction between in-group and foreigner—a distinction that, as we have seen, existed at the earliest times.

This distinction did not survive unsullied for too many centuries. Although edicts and laws continued to assert, more or less, the ille-gality of enslaving members of one's own group, the practice grew and became well established, nurtured by economic hardship on the one hand and the demand for slaves on the other. In China there is clear documentation of this by 200 B.C., and it undoubtedly was not a newly born practice at that time. Wilbur comments:

> . . . the sale of women and children because of economic dis-tress is a constant factor during all Chinese history when slavery was an established institution. Numerous instances of the sale of children from the beginning of Han times through the Ming period appear in the dismal record of famines spread out year by year in the pages of Chinese encyclopedias . . . As late as 1920–21, women and children, particularly young girls, were sold in large number in a north-China famine which cost 500,000 lives. Yet at that time slavery was already legally abolished in China (1943:85).

Periodically, imperial edicts were issued to free those forced into slavery by famine. In 202 B.C., for example, such an edict said: "Those common people who because of famine have sold themselves to be people's male and female slaves are all to be freed and become com-moner" (Wilbur 1943:268).

It is unclear how effectively these edicts were enforced since the practice continued and edicts were repeated. In addition, it would seem that being forced into slavery by indebtedness due to individual, rather than mass, misfortunes was not covered by such edicts.

Foreigners, of course, continued to be a major source of slaves. The blurring of the original distinction and the willingness to enslave others of one's own group, however, was clear. It is, perhaps, best attested to by the practice of kidnapping people, transporting them a few hundred miles, and selling them as slaves. The prevalence of this practice is, perhaps, revealed by an edict of A.D. 9 that denounced kidnapping of people for sale and three edicts in A.D. 31, 36, and 37 ordering that those kidnapped and enslaved were to be freed.

These developments in China occurred independently, indigenously. There was, almost certainly, no contact between the Chinese societies of this time and those of India, western Asia, or southern Europe. So the fact that discussing China has brought us forward in time is not important. But let us go back to western Asia and back in time to before 2,000 B.C. in Mesopotamia to look at how slavery developed there.

Among the tablets uncovered from the time of the third dynasty of Ur there are many that are records of, essentially, court proceedings and judgments. They provide precise information about some aspects of human slavery during this time, about 2,200 B.C. They indicate clearly that slavery, here also, was no longer restricted to foreigners. Economic circumstances and indebtedness brought about the enslavement of own-group members. The following examples, all from Siegel, illustrate the variety of occurrences.

> A certain Ninzagisi said that she was not sold by her father. The witnesses of the sale then give their testimony, upon which Ninzagisi contests their statement. The owner of the purchased maid servant is then made to swear to the purchase, and the girl is confirmed for the purchaser. (1947:12)

> Apparently Namnindu had claimed she had not sold her daughter to Dingirsaga. Dingirsaga, it is said, had bought Nin(x)baba, a maid servant from her mother for her completed price of five shekels silver. Moreover, he brought the tablet (contract) of purchase before the judges. The mother then yields before the testimony and swears not to raise any future claim for the girl. (p. 19).

Clearly, it was legal and ordinary to sell one's children into slavery. There must have been some restrictions, however, on self-sale since such contracts are partly disguised.

> "Completed (case). (Ur)ningišzida . . . and . . . (X)ninmug swore that (E)mulu had bought (Lu)galuruda for the price of 8 shekels from the mother of Lugaluruda; that the price of himself had been filled into Lugaluruda's hand."

The form of the document is clearly that of a contract for sale. Apparently, a legal fiction is used, a self-sale being couched . . . in terms of a parent-child sale. The fact that the mother's name was unmentioned is evidence of the unimportant role she played in the sale. (p. 23)

And another avenue of enslavement also existed.

> In Ur III times, murder of a free man by another free man was a crime punishable not only by death for the culprit but by the enslavement of his entire family. (p. 24)

It is obvious that the distinction between in-group and out-group was no longer absolute. But it had not disappeared: it had only blurred. There were conditions and restrictions on in-group slavery that did not pertain to foreign slaves. There are indications, for example, that a man's family, enslaved because he murdered another man, was enslaved for the purpose of financial compensation and was to be freed when enough years had passed. There are also indications that native slaves were treated differently than foreign slaves and protected from indiscriminate sale, particularly from sale abroad. Siegel summarizes as follows:

> The bulk of the enslaved war captives and slaves acquired in trade undoubtedly fell to the palace and temple, some to the bureaucratic officials. In addition, there was a large body of inland slaves sold out of economic distress. . . . Anyone who could, acquired sources of labor other than his own children. . . . The very frequent claims to freedom on the part of the (inland) slave, in itself, testifies to their mild treatment and to the fact that their status could hardly be distinguished from low-class free laborers and retainers. Such slaves were also protected by the state from sale abroad. . . . Prisoners of war and foreign slaves were characteristically chattels, but the inland slave was differentiated in a number of ways from other forms of property and was considered legally and socially a human being. (1947:49)

Of course, the frequent claims in the courts of inland slaves might also indicate that the distinctions between foreigners and own-group members kept breaking down. There is an assemblage of laws, generally called the Code of Hammurabi, that perhaps casts some light on this. This collection of laws, which dates to about 1900 B.C., has been almost completely reconstructed from the large number of copies that have been found.

This code was neither a complete codification of current law, nor was it a statement of new laws. Indeed, many parts of the Hammurabi Code are nearly identical to fragments of law codes dating two hundred years earlier. It seems that Hammurabi chose to selectively restate principles that had existed for many years in the region. Driver and Miles point out they represented a set of principles to be reaffirmed rather than a set of statutes: "There is not a single case in the thousands of legal documents and reports which have been preserved in which reference is made to the wording of the text of the Laws; indeed, neither judges nor private persons in their documents seem to have regarded it as verbally binding on them" (1952 1:53). According to Driver and Miles: "the subjects with which [Hammurabi] deals are chosen simply because in his opinion they call for amendment or require to be emphasized by republication" (p. 45).

It is significant that a very appreciable portion of the things that Hammurabi presumably thought needed amendment or reemphasis dealt with slavery: slavery was clearly encountering social and legal problems. Of 282 paragraphs in these laws, at least 35 deal with slaves and enslavement. These paragraphs deal with such things as special rights of slave girls who bear sons for their owner, matters of status and inheritance of a free woman who marries a slave, injury to someone else's slave, selling slaves fraudulently, penalties for helping or allowing slaves to escape, liability for actions of a slave, and many others.

Of particular relevance there is the presence among these paragraphs of statements concerning the distinctions between natives and foreigners and restrictions on the enslavement and sale of natives. There are two paragraphs (280 and 281) that affirm that if a slave is bought abroad and, on returning, is revealed to be a native, the purchased slave is automatically declared free. All commentators agree that this is also a reaffirmation of the illegality of selling a native slave abroad. A number of paragraphs concern the conditions of servitude of those seized because of a debt or of family members sold in payment of a debt. There are penalties for ill treatment (paragraphs 115 and 116) and a limitation of three-years duration of slavery for a native (paragraphs 117 and 119).

It is a fair presumption that these various sections represented attempts to deal with recurring problems. Indeed, prohibitions on the sale of native slaves abroad and time limitations with regard to natives sold into slavery because of debt reappear in Assyrian law and in later Hebrew law, although by this later time the period of slavery permitted for a native has become six years rather than three.

Human slavery in ancient societies clearly presented many problems in addition to the growing tendency to enslave natives for debt. The large number of items in the laws of Hammurabi attest to this. There were always troubles connected with human slaves. Humans did not take well to the condition of slavery—for example, they ran away:

> The flight, indeed, of slaves of both sexes seems to have been a common occurrence; for not only do sellers safeguard themselves against the flight or death of slaves in the contract of sale, but there are also documents concerned with their safe custody or return to their owners if taken in flight (Driver and Miles 1952:105–6)

There are also severe penalties for harboring fugitive slaves and rewards for returning them (Mendelsohn 1932).

Attempted escape was not the only problem. The entire history of human slavery through the time of the Roman empire (and probably beyond that, although we have not explored further) is also punctuated with slave rebellions. The general reputation of slaves was that they were poor workers. In addition slaves never seemed to reproduce in adequate numbers. Additional supplies had to be brought in continually by conquest or by trade. If outside sources of new slaves ceased to be available, the slave population always dwindled markedly and rapidly.

Given these problems with human slavery, one may wonder about why it grew more and more prevalent, and why it persisted as a normal and accepted institution for so long. It is very difficult to estimate reliably the size of the slave populations in successive empires—Babylonian, Assyrian, Persian, etc. Sargent (1924), after careful examination of census figures and grain production, estimates that the slave population of Greece in the fifth and fourth centuries B.C. was large indeed. For example, the population of Attica is estimated "in the latter part of the fourth century as consisting of about 93,000 free inhabitants and 60,000 to 70,000 slaves" (p. 128). And other areas, such as Chios and Lacedaemon, probably had even higher proportions of slaves.

During the centuries of dominance by Rome the slave population there was certainly even higher than in ancient Greece. The government administration, industry, mines, and crafts could not have functioned without human slaves (Louis 1965). One cannot say that human slavery was a failure. An institution that increasingly supplied the basic economic motor for three and a half thousand years in western Asia and Europe has to be deemed successful—at least in its time. Slavery declined, particularly in Europe, only when the Roman empire started to weaken and finally the stream of newly captured slaves was reduced to almost nothing.

For our understanding of humans and human society, it must be stressed that human slavery was not only considered normal but was bolstered by religious and moral belief. The Hebrew religion sanctioned human slavery: it only frowned on excessively long enslavement of other Hebrews. The Christian religion also approved of slavery, exhorting slaves to be loyal to their owners. Christianity promised some measure of equality only after death. Religious and moral condemnations of slavery only followed its actual diminution in practice.

Slavery provided a work force—a coerced, troublesome and, often, unreliable one, it is true. But a work force was needed; from the time of the earliest beginnings of agriculture an organized work force was necessary. Grain had to be planted and harvested during short periods of time. Animals had to be cared for, bred, fed, and slaughtered. When dry farming proved to be inadequate, irrigation canals had to be dug and maintained. When metal began to be used, ore had to be mined and smelted.

Who was to do the work? The answer was lesser beings who could be captured or bought or even those who, through indebtedness, could be forced into at least temporary servitude. Human slavery was a solution to the problem of providing the manpower to do the work. When slavery in Europe diminished in importance because slaves were unobtainable, this did not mean that there was in place a more adequate or efficient means of getting work done. The impact on the economy must have been considerable for quite a while, perhaps similar to what one might envision if, over a period of a few hundred years, all farm machinery, mining machinery, and industrial machinery disappeared from the twentieth-century Western world.

CHAPTER THIRTEEN
Reflections on the Present

I HAVE painted a picture of man, the ingenious animal, applying his ingenuity to exploiting and controlling his world, suffering and solving the unanticipated consequences of his actions. It is, to be sure, not a comprehensive picture of the highly complex human animal, but it is one important, undeniable aspect.

The manufacture of tools, the control of fire, and the other early inventions that enabled much more effective exploitation of environmental resources and permitted the species to expand into previously uninhabitable areas had its consequences. For more than a million years the human has been utterly dependent on technology. The species cannot survive without it.

The improvement of hunting tools, the expansion of the variety of usable foods, and the discovery of ways to store foods enabled some groups to settle down and live in one place all year round. This in turn led to serious problems of inevitable large increases in local populations.

Intensive agriculture ensued, increasing the locally available food supply, but introducing greater long-term vulnerability. I have tried to spell out part of the sequence of problem solving and the creation of new problems that led to highly organized, hierarchical societies, organized conflicts among groups, and the necessity of a large, controllable work force. These represent the beginnings of the complicated societal and technological world in which we live today.

To jump from prehistorical and early historical times into the present, we must skip over more than two thousand years of extraordinarily rapid technological and social change. Indeed, the technological, philosophical, moral, and ethical underpinnings of current societies owe much to those millennia we are going to ignore. But to think seriously about classical Greek and Roman societies, the medieval world, and the transformations wrought during the last five hundred years would require several more volumes. The issues we have dealt with, however, have cast some light on the human species and on the whys and hows of some important changes that occurred—at least I think light has been so cast. So from the perspective of what we may have learned, I want to look at the present.

No one has to be reminded that there are large numbers of problems with which individuals and societies live today. A listing of them would make very tedious reading. We cope with them somehow: a few seem to disappear, others merely change their form, while many new problems continue to emerge. The sequence of successive "solutions" to the problems we discussed in the previous chapter is illustrative. It is not clear that human society has ever adequately solved the problem of providing an organized, effective work force. Slavery never totally disappeared, it may still be found here and there today. But conditions changed, and it became more and more a negligible institution. "Free" men, in addition, seemed to work more efficiently and more reliably.

In Europe, during the period of economic decline and population decrease of the early Middle Ages, in the resulting largely agricultural society, the institution of serfdom seemed to serve well. Serfs were not slaves; they were not chattel that could be bought and sold. They were free men who had a personal, mutual bond with and allegiance to their lord. Practices varied widely in different areas and how onerous their obligations were to the lord also varied. They might be obligated to devote some given number of days a week to working for the lord; they could be taxed in various ways by the lord; and the lord frequently had some rights of inheritance.

Serfdom did not last for too long as an effective institution. Its demise had nothing to do with religion, morals, or ethical values. Indeed, the Church was one of the largest employers of serfs in Europe. The system was primarily an agricultural adaptation. The revival of industry and trade in Europe, starting in the twelfth and thirteenth centuries, made the institution ineffective as a provider of a work force for the economy generally. So serfdom dwindled into unimportance, but it is interesting that serfdom was still a legal institution in France until the French Revolution.

More problems arose with the harnessing of water power, wind power and, much later, coal power for industrial purposes. Increasingly, industry could not exist in small, dispersed locations. Sometimes, power could only be effectively harnessed at central locations near the power sources. Again, the problem of providing a work force for these factories was not adequately handled by existing institutions. The English Enclosure Laws provide an interesting example of one way in which one society dealt with this problem. By depriving the small agriculturalist of the possibility of adequate fodder for his farm animals, these laws drove many off the farms and into the factories.

In many ways society has learned to be more clever in how it goes about providing an organized work force. And much has been achieved. During a recent subway and bus strike in the City of New York, in spite of the removal of the major means of transportation in the city, for many days workers exercised ingenuity and patience and engaged in Herculean efforts to go to their jobs every day. Absenteeism was very low—a truly remarkable phenomenon. One cannot imagine a slave population behaving this way.

But in spite of all this, enormously serious problems remain. How does one cope with inefficiency, featherbedding, strikes, seniority systems, and the like? There is some promise of hope, however. A new approach to this age-old problem is well underway and will, inevitably, increase in intensity. The new approach is simple: eliminate the need for a large, organized work force. This new approach is, of course, made possible by modern technology combined with the control that the computer and microprocessors enable.

There are several major indications of this trend. In the United States, at least, more and more banks have "automatic tellers." To withdraw money, one simply goes to a machine, inserts a card, tells the machine how much, and the machine dutifully and accurately counts out and delivers the money. The reliance on human workers is greatly reduced.

New automobile factories in Japan and in the United States have many functions automatically performed by special-purpose robots. The need for human labor is again sharply reduced. And we are on the verge of successful introduction of so-called "intelligent robots"— not the science fiction robot that acts like a human but simply robotic machines that can be preprogrammed to do a variety of tasks as the situation requires.

The orientation of these developments is different, qualitatively, from the orientation of the prior introduction of machinery. Before computer control, machinery was intended to make the human worker more effective and the machinery was designed to be compatible with the human that operated it. With computer control such compatibility is no longer always needed—the human often does not run the machine. Increasingly, the only need will be for highly technical people who can design and build and maintain the machines.

It is no accident that, at least in the United States, there is a serious shortage of workers in such occupations as computer programming and electronic engineering. The major unemployment exists for those with few technical skills. It is also no accident that the large expansion of general employment opportunities has occurred in service occupations such as fast-food restaurants—jobs that require little skill, little training, and in which high turnover of workers is of little consequence—jobs which are obviously lowly paid.

With such revolutionary developments occurring there will undoubtedly be problems created but the end result need not be a picture of poverty and doom. Indeed, some would look forward to an era of potential plenty, relief from labor, and easy lives. But like all new solutions to problems throughout human history and prehistory, new and unforeseen problems will arise in place of those that have been "solved."

We know little about, and have not thought about, the psychological and social conequences of large numbers of humans who, no matter how well provided for they may be, no matter how luxurious their living conditions might become, nevertheless see themselves as useless. How can humans, who have evolved as creative, ingenious, and inventive exploiters and controllers of their environment, adapt to this new kind of world?

Most of us still have faith that human imagination and ingenuity, materialized through technology and new social institutions, will effectively cope with the problems that human societies have inherited and with the new problems that are created. After all, examine the past—a successive series of problems, each in turn successfully solved. That is only one view of the past, however. Another view might contend that each solution produced a change that was irrevocable and that the unforeseen new problems created by these solutions were successively larger in magnitude than the ones disposed of.

Many of us have the remarkable ability to view this endless succession of problems and solutions as progress. There is, indeed, an inclination to view any change that is irrevocable as a step forward. There is not even a useful word in the English language to describe the sequences through the millennia without connotations concerning worse or better. If we stop beguiling ourselves with notions of progress and with images of the nobility of our species, we can look at the past as an extraordinary demonstration of success at coping with problems that arose and as an equally good demonstration of failure in preventing new problems from arising. Clearly, modern human beings have difficulties applying their ingenuity to the future.

One difficulty is that we, as a species, do not have enough imagination. We see and recognize the problems that are already upon us, struggling to find ways to cope with them, but we are very limited in our ability to foresee the new problems that will shortly arrive. Looking into the future usually turns into exaggerations of the present, extrapolations of the past, or vague generalities. I doubt that anyone, for example, in 1920 imagined at all properly about the effect that the mass introduction of the automobile would have on living patterns and population distribution. In retrospect it is easy to see how it affected the growth of suburbs, the decline of cities, the decay of railroads, the locations of factories, and on and on. But in retrospect it is too late to do anything but try to solve the new problems.

Another difficulty is that we, as a species, have an easy time convincing ourselves and each other that our current ethic, morality, and way of living is not just good or better but comes close to being Truth. We, today, regard as barbarous such practices as selective infanticide, sacrifices to pagan gods, or the enslavement of human beings— practices that in earlier times we would have deemed just, honorable, and morally right. The things we do are always good. No one in his right mind would question, for example, the essential goodness of providing medical technology and assistance to people who live in less privileged parts of the world, thus sharply decreasing infant mortality, ensuring a soaring rate of population growth, and thereby virtually condemning a region to long-lasting poverty. There are some parts of the world now where the population, already quite large, is generating new people at a rate that will double its size in thirty years.

A third difficulty is that while, perhaps we are the only existing species capable of sustained logical thought, such thought does not come easy to us. Very few of us ever get very good at it—to most it remains difficult and even alien. The simplest example through which this difficulty may be seen is the learning of arithmetic to which, in highly literate societies, almost all children are exposed. An adequate understanding of arithmetic is never achieved by most people. Try finding some adult who really feels comfortable with fractions. Many who even received excellent grades in the subject in elementary school are baffled if they must add one-third to one-half. They ponder and ponder and some do and most do not remember the relevant rule that they learned by rote.

Schools, of course, largely adapt to this by teaching arithmetic by requiring such rote learning of arbitrary rules and procedures, and such an adaptation is better than nothing. Departures from such a procedure for mass education have not been successful. Not so long ago a wave of the "new math" swept over the schools in the United States. Representing a revulsion against cookbook teaching, it attempted to teach principles so that students would truly understand the relations among numbers. It was a dismal failure. I doubt if very many who were in school during those years recall how to convert a number from base 7, say, to base 3 or even remember what that means. Logical thinking is simply difficult for our species. Perhaps the cheap, hand-held calculator will effectively circumvent the arithmetic problem, but logical thinking is still essential and is a rare commodity.

Toda says that we urgently need a "science of civilization." He fears that the acceleration in technical advances and the accompanying social and societal changes is becoming too much for the individual to cope with adequately. He likens the situation of human society to that of passengers in a "sports car named civilization" (1982:13), automatically accelerating to higher and higher speeds and, gradually, the passengers come to realize that no one knows where the brake pedal or the steering wheel are. The science of civilization is intended to discover the brake and the steering wheel and to learn how to control the car. Or perhaps what such a science would have to do is to manufacture functional brakes and a steering wheel.

From one point of view it is a surprise to find that someone in the year 1982 is calling for a science of civilization. Is this not what the social sciences, collectively, have been working at? What else have psychologists, sociologists, political scientists, economists, anthropologists, and historians been doing other than creating a science of man in his society and a science of the functioning and structure of human society? If Toda is justified in calling for a new science, it must be that the social sciences, whatever they have accomplished that is positive, have failed totally to shed light on how we can do anything about the ever-increasing rate with which we replace old problems with new problems, the process that we insist on calling progress.

To reexamine what we do, how we apply our resourcefulness to the "solutions" of problems and our inability to look further ahead than yesterday, let us take one microcosm of society for illustration, namely, medical practices. It is a good example to take because these practices are not imposed on society by the medical profession; rather they are imposed on that profession by society, and so we can view it as a reflection of the functioning of society, of its values and its goals.

Medicine and its allied, supporting sciences and professions have been phenomenally successful in solving many of the problems that have harassed human beings for centuries and even millennia. Society wants to get rid of disease and illness and, indeed, this has been done in many areas. We no longer have epidemics of Bubonic plague; cholera, once a dread fatal disease, is now rare and easily curable; small pox has disappeared and polio is close to disappearance, to name but a few. For other diseases that still threaten there are ever increasingly effective vaccines to protect us. Our understanding of viruses, bacteria, and toxic substances has enabled us to decrease vastly the death rate associated with birth and childhood and to enable people to live much longer than was possible in earlier eras.

It is impressive. It is not the least of the monuments to the uniquely human attributes of creativity and ingenuity. However, in the process of eradicating disease we have created two new sets of illness: cardiovascular diseases and cancerous diseases. Perhaps "created" is too strong a word. Shall we say "elevated to a state of prominence and prevalence." At a time when very few people lived past the age of forty neither of these afflictions was anything but a rarity. They are both, to a major extent, diseases of old age.

We are, of course, busily engaged in solving these new problems. Each year we identify more and more substances that are carcinogenic which we can avoid. And if one, unfortunately, has a cancer the treatment becomes more effective every decade. The rate of progress in cardiovascular diseases is even more impressive. Fewer and fewer people die from their first "heart attack," and only the other day there was announced the approval of a new drug which strongly reduced the likelihood of a second one. If we do not smoke, are very careful about blood serum cholesterol levels, exercise properly, check our blood pressure levels regularly, and avoid debilitating stress, who knows how much longer one can delay cardiovascular problems. There is no question in my mind that in the not too distant future this disease of old age will have been eliminated as a major cause of death.

But what is it we are after? What do we aim for? As one cynical friend of mine remarked when told of the drug that prevents recurrence of myocardial infarctions: "That's wonderful. That means that one can live a couple of more years and get cancer." But this friend is undoubtedly too cynical for cancer, also, will in time be eradicated.

Are we seriously aiming for immortality? The idea of the total elimination of disease almost implies that we are, but I am quite sure that the social, societal, and economic framework within which we live could not even come close to coping with immortality. I do not think our current institutions and ways of life are compatible even with a life span of 150 years. We seem to be inexorably moving in that direction, however, but we have no vision, no idea, no comprehension of the ethics, moralities, value systems, and institutional structure of a civilization that would be needed to deal with such a change. Without foresight we will solve the problems after they arise and let the new problems inundate us in turn.

If we are not aiming for immortality, then, perhaps, the purpose is simply to eliminate those illnesses which are painful and those that produce death or incapacity in an otherwise well-functioning, highly active person. So we might want to leave untouched whatever existing diseases there are, or new ones that may appear, that only attack people whose functioning has already begun to deteriorate and which produce death painlessly. But obviously, that is not what we want. We could have that now at any person's own option if society wanted that solution. A general societal acceptance of the right of any person to decide when to end his own life, together with the public availability of easy, painless ways to do so, would serve this purpose very nicely. We do not do this, however. Apparently, this is not the purpose—or, more likely, there is no long-run purpose that, collectively, we think about seriously.

For all technologies there is an intimate connection between their development and ensuing changes in value systems and societal structures. Frequently, we see the psychological and social changes that are occurring but have little idea of why they are occurring. There is no need to catalogue all of these: our newspapers tell us every day of growing numbers of single family households, increasing crime rates, the popularity of various drugs, and on and on.

Sometimes we see the growing new technologies but are only dimly aware that the changes they bring about will have social repercussions, the nature of which we do not know. The exploration and use of outer space, the spread of computers and microprocessors, and genetic engineering are only a few examples. On December 13, 1981, the *New York Times* carried, on its front page, an article on the rapid developments in the studies on genes and the practical successes achieved and to be achieved in the near future. The article also refers briefly to the anticipation that these accelerating technical advances are "promising social, economic and philosophical effects that are impossible to predict, but sure to be significant." It illustrates well how we deal with future consequences of technology. The word "promising" has no connotation of warning—indeed it even sounds pleasant. And since prediction is "impossible," we need do nothing more about it. All these achievements fill us with enthusiasm and awe but they should also fill us with worry. Can people and societies change rapidly enough to cope and in what directions should these changes take place? Surely, whatever the shortcomings of our species, we must do the best we can to plan to avoid the new problems. We now do nothing at all.

I realize that I have been talking primarily about large industrialized societies and not about problems of all people everywhere. The problems differ radically, of course, between New York City and a small village in, say, the Sudan. But I do not think these differences can or will last long, perhaps only for another one or two hundred years—a very short period of time.

I am inclined to think that we cannot do much about our lack of foresight and that we will continue to substitute one problem for another. As a species we are severely limited in our cognitive capacities, and these limitations probably prevent us from even asking the right questions. This does not mean doom—it may simply mean an endless frontier of new, difficult problems that we will have to deal with and try to "solve." Perhaps all we can achieve is to get some perspective on the matter from examining the past which, I guess, is what I have been trying to do.

There are some who think that the limitations on our thought processes can be overcome with the assistance of computers. Since computers operate logically, indeed computers insist on operating logically, that human limitation is irrelevant. Since computers have the speed, the capacity, and the patience to examine all possibilities in detail, so the argument goes, the limitations on human imagination may be irrelevant. Jastrow, for example, brings himself to talk about "the human brain, ensconced in a computer, . . . liberated from the weaknesses of the mortal flesh" (1981:166).

To be fair, Jastrow is talking about his image of the future, and I, with my skepticism about the imaginative range of the human mind, only want to talk about the present. But I do not think that the computers that our species can build and program can totally escape the limitations of the human being. We have been able to build and program computers that think logically because our species, or at least some of the members of the species, understand the character of logical thought and are capable of engaging in it even though it is difficult and does not come naturally. We have not produced a computer that thinks imaginatively, however, because we do not understand the characteristics of this kind of thought.

If we look back at what may be considered some of the great imaginative achievements of humans, we can get a picture of how severe our limitations are in this realm. I do not mean to denigrate these achievements—to me they seem truly monumental because I, too, am human. But I will try to describe them in a way that highlights the point I wish to make.

One of the great imaginative accomplishments was that of Copernicus. He obviously realized that if some object changes its position relative to some observer, it could be because one or the other or both had moved. His great imaginative leap was simply to wonder whether or not a system could be constructed in which the sun, rather than the earth he lived on, was assumed to be a stationary center. For a human being this slight reformulation was a difficult thing to conceive and represents extraordinary imagination. Kepler's ensuing great imaginative accomplishment was to consider the possibility that planets moved in eliptical rather than circular paths. And later on, of course, it was a mighty analogical leap to wonder whether all matter looked internally like lots of tiny solar systems.

The thought processes involved in such imaginations, so difficult for man to make, are starkly simple—we could program computers to do such things. We are able to consider the opposite of some proposition—instead of the sun moving around the earth, consider the earth moving around the sun. We are able to consider slight deviations from propositions—instead of a circle consider an elipse, instead of light traveling in straight lines, maybe it travels in slightly curved paths. We are able to play with analogies—tiny little solar systems, electrons flowing in a wire like water flows from a higher to a lower place. But if these are the greatest kinds of imaginative thought that our species can engage in, it is easy to understand our difficulty in looking forward, in anticipating what is going to happen. And these limitations will also, I believe, limit what the computers that we conceive, build, and program can do.

There is an additional aspect to this perspective, however. Species that represent highly complicated life forms do not seem to last very long. In spite of our understandable inclination to regard our own species as the culmination of an evolutionary development, the more likely fact is that Modern man is one more biological stage in an evolutionary sequence. Our predecessors, Homo sapiens, survived for only about 60,000 years. We, as a biological species, have already been around for at least 40,000 years—longer than that if Vandermeersch is correct about the dating of remains from Qafzeh.

A new species, no more different from us than we are from Homo sapiens, if it had greater imagination, a more effective language, and a neural structure that made logical thinking easy and natural, could obviously deal more effectively with the kind of technological civilizations that we have created. It would not require extensive mutations of numerous structural genes to produce such a new species. Probably, it could come about through some seemingly minor changes in the mechanisms for control of gene expression so that a few stages of growth were lengthened, some others shortened. Perhaps, such changes have already occurred here and there.

The question then is, if such genetic change occurred, would a process of natural selection enable this new species to take over, or has modern man already managed to control this process? My own limitations make it impossible for me to answer this question in any way that seems convincing to me. I cannot even clearly discern whether or not any natural selection processes are now operating in the human population or in what direction they may be moving. I hope they are occurring, however. I hope that in five or ten or twenty thousand years a new species of human beings, more able than we, will be around.

References

Allchin, G. 1956. Australian stone industries, past and present. *Royal Anthropological Institute Journal*, 87:115–36.

Bahn, P. G. 1978. The unacceptable face of the west European Upper Paleolithic. *Antiquity*, 52:183–92.

Bahn, P. G. 1980. Reply. *Antiquity*, 54:140–42.

Bar-Yosef, O. 1980. Prehistory of the Levant. *Annual Review of Anthropology*, 9:101–33.

Bar-Yosef, O. 1982. The Mediterranean Levantine Epi-Paleolithic as the background of the "Neolithic revolution." In P. Sorenson and P. Mortenson, eds., *The Origins of Agriculture and Technology*, in press.

Bar-Yosef, O. and B. Vandermeersch. 1981. Notes concerning the possible age of the Mousterian layers in Qafzeh cave. Unpublished ms.

Beck, B. B. 1980. *Animal Tool Behavior*. New York: Garland STPM Press.

Bergounious, F. M. 1961. Notes on the mentality of primitive man. In S. L. Washburn, ed., *Social Life of Early Man*. Viking Fund Publications in Anthropology, no. 31. New York: Wenner Gren Foundation.

Berndt, R. M. and C. Berndt. 1964. *The World of the First Australians*. Chicago: University of Chicago Press.

Binford, L. R. 1968. Post-Pleistocene adaptations. In L. R. Binford and S. R. Binford, eds., *New Perspectives in Archeology*. Chicago: University of Chicago Press.

Blake, W. O. 1858. *The History of Slavery and the Slave Trade*. Columbus, Ohio: J. and H. Miller.

Bordes, F. 1968. *The Old Stone Age*. New York: McGraw-Hill.

Bordes, F. and D. Sonnerville-Bordes. 1970. The significance of variability in Paleolithic assemblages. *World Archaeology*, 2:16–73.

Braidwood, R. J. and B. Howe. 1960. *Prehistoric Investigations in Iraqi Kurdistan*. Studies in Ancient Oriental Civilization, no. 31. Chicago: University of Chicago Press.

Braidwood, R. J., H. Cambel, C. L. Redman, and P. J. Watson. 1971. Beginnings of village-farming communities in southeastern Turkey. *Proceedings of the National Academy of Sciences*, 68:1236–40.

Brain, C. K. 1981. *The Hunters or the Hunted*. Chicago: University of Chicago Press.

Breuil, H. 1952. *Four Hundred Centuries of Cave Art*. Montignac: Centre d' étude et documentation préhistorique.

Burr, D. 1976. Further evidence concerning speech in Neanderthal man. *Man*, n.s. 11:104–10.

Butzer, K. W. 1977. Environment, culture, and human evolution. *American Scientist*, 65:572–84.

Butzer, K. W. 1980. Comments on Wreschner's article on red ochre and human evolution. *Current Anthropology*, 21:635.

Cauvin, J. 1978. Les premiers villages de Syria-Palestine du IXéme au VIIéme millénaire avant J.C. Collection de la maison de l'Orient Mediterranée Ancien, no. 4., Serie Archeologique 3, Lyon.

Chagnon, N. A. and R. B. Hames. 1979. Protein deficiency and tribal warfare in Amazonia: new data. *Science*, 203:910–13.

Chattopadhyay, K. P. 1970. *Ancient Indian Culture Contact and Migrations*. Calcutta: Mukhopadhyay.

Clutton-Brock, J. 1969. Carnivore remains from the excavations of the Jericho Tell. In P. J. Ucko and G. W. Dimbleby, eds., *The Domestication and Exploitation of Plants and Animals*. Chicago: Aldine.

Cohen, M. N. 1977. *The Food Crisis in Prehistory*. New Haven: Yale University Press.

Cowgill, G. L. 1975. On the causes and consequences of ancient and modern population changes. *American Anthropologist*, 77:505–25.

Dart, R. A. and P. B. Beaumont. 1971. On a further radiocarbon date for ancient mining in southern Africa. *South African Journal of Science*, 67:10–11.

Davis, S. and F. Valla. 1978. Evidence for the domestication of the dog 12,000 years ago in the Natufian of Israel. *Nature*, 276:608–10.

de Lumley, H. 1971. L'homme de Tautarel. *Courrier* (CNRS), 2:16–20.

de Lumley, H. 1975. Cultural evolution in France in its paleoecological setting during the Middle Pleistocene. In K. W. Butzer and G. LL. Isaac, eds., *After the Australopithecines*. The Hague: Mouton.

de Lumley, H. and Y. Boone. 1976. Les structures d'habitat au Paléolithique. Inférieur. In H. de Lumley, ed., *La Préhistoire Francaise*, vol. 1. Paris: CNRS.

Diakonoff, I. M. 1958. Some remarks on the "reforms" of Urukagina. *Revue d'Assyriologie et d'archeologie orientale*, 52:1–15.

Dixon, J. R. 1976. Obsidian characterization studies in the Mediterranean and Near East. In R. E. Taylor, ed., *Advances in Obsidian Glass Studies*. Park Ridge, N.J.: Noyes Press.

Dorell, P. 1978. The uniqueness of Jericho. In R. Moorey and P. Parr, eds., *Archaeology in the Levant*. Warminster, Eng.: Aris and Phillips.

Driver, G. R. and J. C. Miles. 1952. *The Babylonian Laws*. 2 vols. Oxford: Clarendon Press.

Drower, M. S. 1969. The domestication of the horse. In P. J. Ucko and G. W. Dimbleby, eds., *The Domestication and Exploitation of Plants and Animals*. Chicago: Aldine.

Erman, A. 1894. *Life in Ancient Egypt.* London: Macmillan.

Flannery, K. V. 1969. Origins and ecological effects of early domestication in Iran and the Near East. In P. J. Ucko and G. W. Dimbleby, eds., *The Domestication and Exploitation of Plants and Animals.* Chicago: Aldine.

Flannery, K. V. 1972. The origins of the village as a settlement type. In P. Ucko, R. Tringham, and G. W. Dimbleby, eds., *Man, Settlement, and Urbanism.* London: Duckworth.

Fortea Perez, F. J. 1975. Algunas aportaciones a los porblemas del arte levantino. *Zephyrus,* 24:225–57.

Freeman, L. G. 1973. The significance of mammalian fauna from Paleolithic occupations in Cantabrian Spain. *American Antiquity,* 38:3–34.

Freeman, L. G. 1975. Acheulian sites and stratigraphies in Iberia and the Maghreb. In K. W. Butzer and G. LL. Isaac, eds., *After the Australopithecines.* The Hague: Mouton.

Gadd, C. J. 1970. The cities of Babylonia. In *The Cambridge Ancient History,* 1:2. Cambridge: Cambridge University Press.

Garrod, D. A. E. and D. M. Bate. 1937. *The Stone Age of Mount Carmel,* vol. 1. Oxford: Oxford University Press.

Gerstang, J. 1953. *Prehistoric Mersin.* Oxford: Oxford University Press.

Gimbutas, M. 1974. *The Gods and Goddesses of Old Europe.* Berkeley: University of California Press.

Gokhale, B. G. 1952. *Ancient India: History and Culture.* London: Asia Publishing House.

Graziosi, P. 1960. *Paleolithic Art.* New York: McGraw Hill.

Hahn, J. 1972. Das aurignacien in mittel und ost-Europa. *Acta Praehistorica et Archeologica,* 3:77–107.

Hallo, W. W. and J. J. A. Van Dijk. 1968. *The Exaltation of Inanna.* New Haven: Yale University Press.

Harlan, J. R. 1967. A wild wheat harvest in Turkey. *Archaeology,* 20:197–201.

Harrold, F. B. 1980. A comparative analysis of Eurasian Paleolithic burials. *World Archaeology,* 12:195–210.

Hawkes, J. G. 1969. The ecological background of plant domestication. In P. J. Ucko and G. W. Dimbleby, eds., *The Domestication and Exploitation of Plants and Animals.* Chicago: Aldine.

Helbaek, J. 1969. Ecological effects of irrigation in ancient Mesopotamia. In P. J. Ucko and G. W. Dimbleby, eds., *The Domestication and Exploitation of Plants and Animals.* Chicago: Aldine.

Henin, R. A. 1969. Patterns and causes of fertility differentials in the Sudan. *Population Studies,* 23:171–98.

Ho, Ping-ti. 1975. *The Cradle of the East.* Chicago: University of Chicago Press.

Holloway, R. 1974. The casts of fossil hominid brains. *Scientific American,* 231(1):106–15.

References

Howell, F. C. 1966. Observations on the earlier phases of the European Lower Paleolithic. *American Anthropologist*, 68(2/2):88–201.

Howells, W. W. 1975. Neanderthal man: Facts and figures. In R. H. Tuttle, ed., *Australopithecus Paleoanthropology: Morphology and Paleoecology*. The Hague: Mouton.

James, B. O. 1957. *Prehistoric Religion*. London: Thames and Hudson.

Jastrow, R. 1981. *The Enchanted Loom*. New York: Simon and Schuster.

Jelinek, A. 1977. The Lower Paleolithic: current evidence and interpretations. *Annual Review of Anthropology*, 6:11–32.

Jerison, H. 1973. *Evolution of the Brain and Intelligence*. New York: Academic Press.

Johanson, D. 1980. *Lucy: the Beginnings of Humankind*. New York: Simon and Schuster.

Johanson, D. and T. D. White. 1979. A systematic assessment of early African hominids. *Science*, 203:321–30.

Kawai, M. 1965. Newly acquired precultural behavior of the natural troop of Japanese monkeys on Koshima Islet. *Primates*, 6:1–30.

Kenyon, K. 1957. *Digging up Jericho*. London: Ernest Benn.

Kenyon, K. 1960. Excavations at Jericho, 1957–58. *Palestine Exploration Quarterly*, 92:88–113.

Kirkbride, D. 1968. Beidha: early Neolithic village life south of the Dead Sea. *Antiquity*, 42:263–74.

Klein, R. G. 1973. *Ice-Age Hunters of the Ukraine*. Chicago: University of Chicago Press.

Klein, R. G. 1975. Ecology of Stone Age Man at the southern tip of Africa. *Archaeology*, 28:238–47.

Köhler, W. 1927. *The Mentality of Apes*. London: Rutledge and Kegan Paul.

Kozlowski, J. K. and H. Kubiak. 1972. Late Paleolithic dwellings made of mammoth bones in south Poland. *Nature*, 237:463–64.

Kozlowski, J. 1972–73. The origin of lithic raw material in the Paleolithic of the Carpathian countries. *Acta Archeologica Carpathica*, 13:5–19.

Kramer, S. N. 1963. *The Sumerians*. Chicago: University of Chicago Press.

Kurten, B. 1965. The carnivora of the Palestine caves. *Acta Zoologica Fennica*, 107:1–74.

Leakey, L. S. B. 1958. Recent discoveries at Olduvai Gorge, Tanganyika. *Nature*, 19:1099–1103.

Lee, R. 1979. *The !Kung San: Men, Women, and Work in a Foraging Society*. Cambridge: Cambridge University Press.

Lee, R. B. and I. DeVore, eds. 1968. *Man the Hunter*. Chicago: Aldine.

Le May, M. 1975. The language capability of Neanderthal man. *American Journal of Physical Anthropology*, 42:9–14.

Lewin, R. 1981. Ethiopian stone tools are world's oldest. *Science*, 211:806–7.

Lewis, B. 1980. *The Sargon Legend*. Dissertation series #4. Cambridge, Mass.: American Schools of Oriental Research.

Lieberman, P. 1975. *On the Origins of Language.* New York: Macmillan.

Lieberman, P. and E. S. Crelin. 1971. On the speech of Neanderthal man. *Linguist Inquiry,* 2:203–22.

Louis, P. 1965. *Ancient Rome at Work.* New York: Barnes and Noble.

Lovejoy, C. O. 1981. The origin of man. *Science,* 211:341–50.

Mallowan, M. E. L. 1970. The development of cities from Al-'Ubaid to the end of Uruk. In *The Cambridge Ancient History,* 1:1. Cambridge: Cambridge University Press.

Mallowan, M. E. L. and R. J. Cruikshank. 1935. Prehistoric Assyria: the excavations at Tell Arpachiyah. *Iraq,* 2(1) London.

Maringer, J. 1960. *The Gods of Prehistoric Man.* London: Weidenfeld and Nicholson.

Marshack, A. 1976. Some implications of the Paleolithic symbolic evidence for the origin of language. *Current Anthropology,* 17:274–81.

Mellaart, J. 1962. Excavations at Çatal Hüyük. *Anatolian Studies,* 12:41–65.

Mellaart, J. 1966. Excavations at Çatal Hüyük, 1965. *Anatolian Studies,* 16:67–110.

Mellaart, J. 1967. *Çatal Hüyük.* New York: McGraw-Hill.

Mellaart, J. 1970a. The earliest settlements in Western Asia from the 9th to the 5th Millennia B.C. In *The Cambridge Ancient History,* 1:1. Cambridge: Cambridge University Press.

Mellaart, J. 1970b. *Excavations at Hacilar.* Edinburgh: Edinburgh University Press.

Mellaart, J. 1975. *The Neolithic of the Near East.* London: Thames and Hudson.

Mendelsohn, I. 1932. *Legal Aspects of Slavery in Babylonia, Assyria, and Palestine.* Williamsport, Pa.: Bayard Press.

Menzel Jr., E. W. 1972. Spontaneous invention of ladders in a group of young chimpanzees. *Folia Primatoligica,* 17:87–106.

Napier, J. 1962. The evolution of the hand. *Scientific American,* 207:56–62.

Pericot, L. and E. R. Ripoll. 1964. *Prehistoric Art of the Western Mediterranean and the Sahara.* Viking Fund Publications in Anthropology, no. 39. New York: Wenner Gren Foundation.

Perrot, J. 1963. Excavations at 'Eynan. *Israel Exploration Journal,* 13:14–22.

Phillips, P. 1980. *The Prehistory of Europe.* Bloomington: Indiana University Press.

Reed, C. A. 1969. The pattern of animal domestication in the prehistoric Near East. In P. J. Ucko and G. W. Dimbleby, eds., *The Domestication and Exploitation of Plants and Animals.* Chicago: Aldine.

Roper, M. K. 1969. A survey of evidence of intra-human killing in the Pleistocene. *Current Anthropology,* 10:427–59.

Rosengarten, Y. 1959. La nation sumerienne de souferainte divine. *Revue de l'histoire des religions,* 156:129–60.

Safar, F. 1949. The identification of Dudu. *Sumer,* 5:133–35.

Sargent, R. K. 1924. *The Size of the Slave Population at Athens During the Fifth and Fourth Centuries Before Christ,* vol. 12. University of Illinois Studies in the Social Sciences. Urbana: University of Illinois Press.

Schaefer, O. 1971. When the Eskimo comes to town. *Nutrition Today,* 6:8–16.

Siegel, B. J. 1947. Slavery during the third dynasty of Ur. *American Anthropologist* n.s., 49(1/2):5–54.

Smith, P. 1972. Diet and attrition in the Natufians. *American Journal of Physical Anthropology,* 37:233–38.

Solecki, R. S. 1959. Three adult Neanderthal skeletons from Shanidar Cave, northern Iraq. *Smithsonian Institution Annual Report,* pp. 603–35.

Solecki, R. S. 1971. *Shanidar: The First Flower People.* New York: Knopf.

Sturdy, D. A. 1975. Some reindeer economies in prehistoric Europe. In E. S. Higgs, ed., *Paleoeconomy.* Cambridge: Cambridge University Press.

Sussman, R. M. 1972. Child transport, family size, and increase in human population during the Neolithic. *Current Anthropology,* 13:258–59.

Thoma, A. 1976. Le peuplement anté-néandertalien d'Europe dans le context paléoanthropologique de l'ancien monde. IX Congress UISPP, Nice. 9:7–16. Paris: CNRS.

Toda, M. 1982. *Man, Robot, and Society.* Boston: Martinus Nijhoff.

Trinkaus, E. 1978. Hard times among the Neanderthals. *Natural History,* 87:58–63.

Vandermeersch, B. 1978. Quelques aspects du probleme de l'origine de l'homme moderne. In *Les Origine Humaine et les Époque de l'Intelligence.* Fondation Singer-Polignac. Paris: Masson.

Van Loon, M. 1968. The oriental institute excavations at Mureybit, Syria. *Journal of Near Eastern Studies,* 27:265–82.

Van Zeist, W. 1976. On macroscopic traces of food plants in southwestern Asia. *Philosophical Transactions, Royal Society London,* series B, 275:27–41.

Vial, L. G. 1940. Stone axes of Mount Hagen. *Oceania,* 11:158–63.

Watson, P. J. 1966. Clues to Iranian prehistory in modern village life. *Expedition,* 8(3):9–19.

Wendorf, F. 1968. A Nubian final Paleolithic graveyard near Jebel Sahaba, Sudan. In F. Wendorf, ed., *The Prehistory of Nubia.* Dallas, Texas: Southern Methodist University Press.

Wendorf, F. and R. Schild. 1980. *Prehistory of the Eastern Sahara.* New York: Academic Press.

Wenke, R. J. 1980. *Patterns in Prehistory.* New York: Oxford University Press.

White, T. D. 1980. Evolutionary implications of Pliocene hominid footprints. *Science,* 208:175–76.

Wilbur, C. M. 1943. *Slavery in China During the Former Han Dynasty.* New York: Russell and Russell.

Wooley, L. 1954. *Excavations at Ur.* New York: Barnes and Noble.

Wreschner, E. E. 1980. Red ochre and human evolution: A case for discussion. *Current Anthropology,* 21:631–33.

Wynn, T. 1979. The intelligence of later Acheulian hominids. *Man,* 14(3):371–91.

INDEX